Praise for *Be Transform*

"*Be Transformed* is a 7-week, step by step guide to emotional and spiritual health. It will guide you from toxic thoughts and emotional wounds from your past into inner healing. Through daily lessons and personal application process, this book helps one to transform their life and relationships.

Be Transformed workbook is an incredible resource that can help one capture and embrace God's vision for your life — a vision that is far more profound than one could ever dream or imagine. With just 10 minutes a day, you will be prompted to look to God's Word for strength and wisdom. This book clearly outlines the biblical solutions for our struggles with guilt, depression, anxiety, and the many issues we struggle with. It gets to the barriers that get in the way of our ability to achieving our goals and outlines the skills we need to grow in all areas leading to a strong and healthy life and our relationships with others. This book will help you form a strong foundation of faith and confidence and help you reflect on how His wisdom can be used to heal and transform your life."

Karen Schadrack, Licensed Therapist

"Change is what counselors are trying to help clients with. Preachers are hoping the Holy Spirit will 'convict' parishioners to change. La Vonne Earl sees change as Transformation. Early on she says, "Change your mind, transform your life." Once again, La Vonne has given us a much-needed tutorial in how to facilitate change. And once again it is sound Biblical advice, made plain with practical applications, in an easy to understand manual. Mrs. Earl, 'Makes it Plain' so we may 'run with it" (Habakkuk 2:2). We are invited by God to act; and La Vonne shows us how in a well-planned, easy to follow *7 Weeks to a New Improved You*. The 7 Weeks are critical as transformative change is a process. Accepting Christ as our Savior is a one-time decision with eternal consequences. Sanctification is a daily decision of transformation. La Vonne readily understands that it is necessary to know Jesus personally so we can recognize His Holy Spirit as our companion on the journey. As you journey on these 7 Weeks, it is my prayer that you will allow a holistic approach of sanctification mentioned in Thessalonians 5:23, "May God himself, the God of peace, sanctify you through and through. May your whole spirit, soul and body be kept blameless at the coming of our Lord Jesus Christ." La Vonne always provides biblical references in her appendices. Her *I AM* references are nearly a concordance. This book is another valuable contribution for your bookshelf and is great for all, including pastors, counselors, home groups, or individual quiet times. Thank You La Vonne for continuing to feed His Sheep."

Houston Ray Johnson, Jr. M.Div. C.P.E.
Chaplain, Tustin Veterans Out Post

"'Being Transformed' is a continual process. I am so grateful for this book which has taken me deeper into my transformation in each area of my life. I like the evaluation tool and the other tools, including anchoring, which has helped me to renew my mind and live from a place of joy, peace, empowerment, and success. I highly recommend this book to anyone!"

Karen Gilbert, Life Coach

"In *Be Transformed*, La Vonne gives biblical tools to grow one's faith in the six key areas of life. Our emotional well-being is found by having a sound mind which is given in God's word. In this workbook you will find biblical guidelines to replace the enemy's lies with the truth, thus helping one develop healthy relationships. I love the practical guidance on how to renew the mind by reframing with a biblical perspective, thus bringing restoration and healing to reclaim one's life. *Be Transformed* is a great resource to help people transform negative thought patterns into a Godly perspective and get into the sweet place of growing closer to our Heavenly Father and His will for our life."

Debbie Hamilton, Marriage by God Counseling President

"La Vonne is an incredible coach that knows how to relate to you and help you to rise into your full potential. She truly has been the hands and feet of Jesus in my life and is an incredibly gifted teacher. I have enjoyed reading *Be Transformed* and found the tools she supplies helpful. As someone that wanted to deepen my relationship with the Lord and improve my life, I can tell you that this book helped me to do just that. I have learned that evaluating one's life is an ongoing process and I have learned how to be more keenly aware of what is going on in each area. I highly recommend this book to everyone."

Carolyn Saucedo, Follower of Jesus Christ

"The *Be Transformed* workbook is an invitation to examine the six key areas of one's life for the purpose of achieving an abundant, meaningful, and joyful life. In this book you will learn the skill of routinely examining your soul and life, knowing Christ is with you to transform any area where needed most. One step at a time, you will gain access to new ways of thinking and behaving, leading you into an intimate relationship with God's Spirit which transforms all our lives bringing us and others more peace and joy."

Tonyah Dee, Author of *How to Meditate with Jesus*

"Real change begins with renewing your mind and La Vonne Earl shows us how practical and easy it is to do so. This resource is full of powerful tools that will help you get the breakthrough you are looking for in any area of life."

Meliza Farndell, Author of *Untangled*

"Gaining a deeper understanding of God's desire for our life in each area helps us to live within God's will. La Vonne does not advise personally but uses God's Word to show how one can coach themselves with their ultimate life coach, Jesus Christ, to improve their life. This was very helpful for me as I have found the Bible to be complicated at times. The real tools La Vonne offers, like how to do an evaluation on yourself or how to practice godly anchoring and visualization, helped me to feel God's grace and yearn for His ways. Even if you think you know everything about the Bible, I highly recommend this book to help you renew your mind in Christ."

Zoey Carpenter, Crossing Cultures, Zimbabwe

Be TRANSFORMED

7 Weeks to a New, Improved You!

La Vonne Earl

Be transformed by the renewing of your mind

Be Transformed: 7 Weeks to a New, Improved You!

Copyright ©2022 by La Vonne Earl

All rights reserved. This book or any portion thereof may not be reproduced or used in any manner whatsoever without the express written permission of the publisher except for the use of brief quotations in a book review.

Published by Kingdom Press Publishing

Book Design: Clarity Designworks

Paperback ISBN: 978-0-9855382-3-1
Ebook ISBN: 978-0-9855382-4-8

Unless otherwise noted, all scripture quotations are taken from *The Passion Translation®* and are marked (TPT). Copyright © 2017, 2018 by Passion & Fire Ministries, Inc. Used by permission. All rights reserved. ThePassionTranslation.com.

Scripture quotations marked (ESV) are taken from the *ESV® Bible (The Holy Bible, English Standard Version®)*, copyright © 2001 by Crossway, a publishing ministry of Good News Publishers. Used by permission. All rights reserved.

Scripture quotations marked (MSG) are taken from *THE MESSAGE*, copyright © 1993, 2002, 2018 by Eugene H. Peterson. Used by permission of NavPress. All rights reserved. Represented by Tyndale House Publishers, a Division of Tyndale House Ministries.

Scripture quotations marked (NKJV) are taken from the New King James Version®. Copyright © 1982 by Thomas Nelson. Used by permission. All rights reserved.

Scripture quotations marked (NIV) are taken from the *Holy Bible, New International Version®, NIV®*. Copyright © 1973, 1978, 1984, 2011 by Biblica, Inc.™ Used by permission of Zondervan. All rights reserved worldwide. www.zondervan.com. The "NIV" and "New International Version" are trademarks registered in the United States Patent and Trademark Office by Biblica, Inc.™

Scripture quotations marked (NLT) are taken from the *Holy Bible, New Living Translation*, copyright ©1996, 2004, 2015 by Tyndale House Foundation. Used by permission of Tyndale House Publishers, a Division of Tyndale House Ministries, Carol Stream, Illinois 60188. All rights reserved.

NOTE: All names in any stories told, and some details of the stories, have been changed to protect the identities of those involved.

I dedicate this book to my brothers and sisters in Christ
who have joined their spirit with Lord and have become one with Him.
May your life continually Be Transformed.

"But the one who joins himself to the Lord is mingled into one spirit with him."
1 Corinthians 6:17 TPT

Contents

Foreword 9

Acknowledgments 11

How to Use This Book 13

Introduction:
   Change Your Mind, Transform Your Life 15

Week One: From Glory to Glory:
   Growing and Being Transformed into His Image 19

Week Two: Spirituality 49

Week Three: Relationships 81

Week Four: Emotional Wellness 109

Week Five: Physical Health and Wellness 135

Week Six: Career and Ministry 161

Week Seven: Finances 189

A Final Word 215

Appendix 217

Foreword

Thinking is an incredible activity. We do it all the time automatically. Scientists say we never stop having words move through our minds. Even when we are asleep, a flow of words is streaming around inside of us. In fact, while human beings can speak at the rate of 150 to 200 words per minute, we think at the rate of 1300 to 1800 words per minute, and we read from 200 to 400 words per minute on average. This helps explain why our mind sometimes wanders when we are listening to someone speaking! Both heaven and hell can invade our thoughts. Our thoughts define us, but they can also refine us if we will allow God to be attached to our mind.

What thoughts fill your heart today? Since our thoughts are programming our lives at the rate of 1300 to 1800 words per minute, 24 hours a day, it is extremely important what kind of thoughts we allow in our minds. If we are constantly getting negative input, our programming is going to be largely negative, which, in turn, will hinder our ability to live happy, healthy lives. Check out those 1300 to 1800 words that are streaming through your mind every minute. Are they building your life...or tearing it down? It seems that every person is divided between a healthy attitude toward themselves that is goal-directed and life-affirming and a destructive side of themselves that can be self-critical, self-denying, and suspicious. This inner critic, or the "critical inner voice" can take over our thinking and lead to a negative cycle of circular thinking and depression. God's answer is to have our minds made new by the life of Christ within us.

It's time to *Be Transformed!*

True transformation begins and ends with our thoughts. We are told throughout Scripture to set our "minds" on things above, to "think" about what is pleasant, peaceable, and pure. We fix our "thoughts" on the One who was crucified in our place so that our minds will be renewed. Yes, God wants to begin with a new you. He will take our NEW life in Christ and filter it through every part of our being, our heart, our emotions, and our thoughts. I am so glad my thoughts can be containers for love, for joy, for blessings, and for God.

Jesus once whispered to me, "If you change your mind, I will change your life."

I believe that LaVonne Earl has discovered the keys to change your life. It begins by changing your thoughts. Imagine if our thoughts were continually fixed on Jesus. How different our lives would be. Instead of negativity, self-hatred, and inner strife, we would be filled with holiness and love. I want my mind renewed, don't you?

La Vonne Earl has given us a practical yet deep road map into soul transformation. Her many years of experience and coaching others has dredged a deep river for us to come and drink from. I'm grateful for the skill and insight by which LaVonne has written this book. You need it. I need it. We all need to Be Transformed! Get ready for a new mindset to guide your life, the mind of Christ.

Brian Simmons, Passion & Fire Ministries

Acknowledgments

To write a book is an incredible team effort. This book was birthed from teaching students at the OC Rescue Mission. I am grateful for each student who gave inspiration on what they needed help with to grow into their godly identity.

I would like to thank Michele Chiappetta for working with my teachings and writings to skillfully compile this workbook. Her passion for the Lord and her desire to see lives *transformed* made it such a pleasure to work with her.

I'd like to thank my sweet husband for supporting me and being my biggest fan, thank you for sacrificing the time we could be together so I could write to help others.

Thank you to Carla Green for the beautiful way you format my book, make additional edits and pull things together, I appreciate you.

Thank you to all my friends and supporters who read this manuscript, offered your feedback, gave reviews, and continually cheered me on to the finish line! Thank you! I am grateful to do life with you!

How to Use This Book

Be Transformed is a seven-week interactive coaching course designed to help you achieve healthy balance and good, godly transformation as you discover how to effectively put into practice biblical truths in the six key areas of your life—spirituality, relationships, emotional wellness, physical health, career/ministry, and finances. Through study and implementation of the concepts, tools, and activities in this book, you will learn how to develop a new and healthy inner narration—a positive, godly way of thinking and speaking to yourself that is based on healthy beliefs and biblical truths about who you are in Christ.

As you grow in these concepts and make use of them daily, you will experience a miraculous transformation! You'll begin to experience life as God intends it—so you can enjoy the sound mind and purposeful life He has for all His children. You'll be better able to walk consistently in His joy, peace, strength and all the many blessings He offers those who are in Him.

Weekly Activities

Each section of this book includes an activities section to guide you daily on your road to self-discovery and transformation so that you can be more like Jesus! These activities are designed to make it easier to learn about yourself, become aware of your current truths, and understand clearly what you'd like to accomplish as you grow in the Lord. Through this path of discovery, you can more easily set goals and make plans that take you in the direction you want to go. This intentional mode of living equips you to take the active daily steps that lead you to be transformed more and more into the image of Christ.

After seven weeks in the class for *Be Transformed*, you will have begun to truly experience what it means to enjoy the perfection of God in each area. It's not that we are perfect, or that we will become perfect in seven weeks, but that He perfects that which concerns us (Psalm 138:8), so that we can enjoy His goodness and glory in the midst of our everyday activities. You'll come to understand and appreciate His perfect will for you in each area of life.

Also, by the end of this course, you will have memorized 43 scriptures—one during the first week as you set goals, and then 42 more scriptures—which is one verse per day for the next six weeks. These verses focus on the concepts you are learning daily in the course, and taken together, they form a strong starting point for you to ground yourself in what God says is true about you. On this firm biblical foundation, you will be better equipped to grow and thrive in Him—which is His greatest desire for you.

Throughout this book, I have used *The Passion Translation* (TPT) for scriptures wherever possible and have used other versions of the Bible for scriptures in cases where *The Passion Translation* has not been completed. I love multiple versions of the Bible, but I find *The Passion Translation* to express the heart of the Lord to its fullness.

There is also a section in each day's activities where you will write a "new narration" for yourself. You will have opportunities to add to it as you continue to set new goals throughout this course and beyond.

Your narration is a positive, faith-filled, encouraging, focused way to speak to yourself about who you are in Christ. This tool can be highly personalized to reflect who God has created you to be, the truth about how He sees you and desires you to see yourself, along with your personal goals and purposes. As you grow in the practice of speaking to yourself the way God speaks—with the voice of victory and love—you'll find yourself strengthened to move forward into greater and greater success in Him.

In the Appendix, there are examples you can use as inspiration as you learn to write your own new narration. Through creating a personalized, godly narration and using it daily, you will develop a new way of seeing and speaking to yourself—not as others have labeled you, or even in any negative ways you may have thought of yourself, but as a beloved child of God. This activity is therefore a powerful, practical way to truly renew your mind (Romans 12:2), which is what leads to true, lasting, godly transformation.

Designed for Individual or Group Discovery

This *Be Transformed* course is designed to be used either alone or in group classes. Whether you are participating in a group or reading the book on your own, the process for engaging with the material here is similar.

You will read one chapter a week and apply the chapter's tools and techniques to your life. Each week is focused on one of the six areas of life and features daily activities—including a scripture a day to memorize as well as homework, usually in the form of questions to answer, and then gleaning from your answers the words God would say to you to add to your godly narration.

As you do the work each day, I encourage you to prayerfully engage with what you are learning, believing God to completely transform your life!

If you are facilitating a group that is studying this book, remember that everyone has different comfort levels with what they may want to share publicly. Encourage everyone in the group to support one another, speak positively to one another, and be patient and accepting. It is not necessary that everyone share personal experiences with the group, and you may wish to remind your group weekly that they never need share anything that causes themselves or others discomfort.

If you'd like to supplement this book with the videos from the live *Be Transformed* class in addition to other materials, please visit www.YKIcoaching.com to discover our positive and practical videos, courses, one-on-one coaching, and other valuable resources. Or email our ministry with your questions: info@YKIcoaching.com.

Introduction: Change Your Mind, Transform Your Life

Welcome to "Be Transformed."

I am so glad you are reading this book! I am excited to take this journey with you as you commit yourself to Christ and allow the Holy Spirit to transform your mind, which is the key to enjoying great success in every area of your life. The good things that God has for you as His beloved child are well worth being dedicated to—and I encourage you to consider this course as a divinely set appointment for you to grow in Him and walk more fully in the destiny He has planned *specifically for you*.

As you take this seven-week journey, you will learn the methods and tools that our ministry uses when coaching others. These techniques will equip you to begin coaching yourself to godly success as you walk daily with the Lord.

As you take this seven-week journey, you will learn the methods and tools that our ministry uses when coaching others. These *techniques* will equip you to begin coaching yourself to godly success as you walk daily with the Lord.

Using Psalm 139:23–24 as your master guide, you will ask God to search your heart and reveal areas in your life that need attention so you can experience positive change. As you come to know greater truth, you will discover places where you can grow even stronger in Him and see greater fruit blossoming from your faith.

Remember, God desires for you to come to Him so He can help you find freedom, accomplish your goals, and be a blessing in every area of life. He is faithful, and He loves guiding His children toward what is good and godly! As you diligently search yourself and look to Him, He will give you the answers you are seeking.

As you begin this course of study with me, I may not personally know where you are in your spiritual walk, what trials you have gone through, or what you are currently facing. I may not be aware of the celebrations you are experiencing, or your heart's desire and goals. *But you do—and God does too!* He will help you as you open up your life to Him, through the techniques shared here, so that you can build on your daily growth in Him and His Word.

Your Kingdom Inheritance—You Know It

"A thief has only one thing in mind—he wants to steal, slaughter, and destroy. But I have come to give you everything in abundance, more than you expect— life in its fullness until you overflow!"
John 10:10 (TPT)

At YKI coaching, the acronym YKI stands for *Your Kingdom Inheritance*. We believe every person has an inheritance from the Lord, and so we desire for you to receive that inheritance. God wants good things for you. Remember, it's the thief who steals, kills, and destroys, but it's God who desires for you to have the abundant life.

You are designed to have a full, healthy, good life. In every area of living, God wants to restore and bless you. To facilitate this process of transformation and blessing, we will take one area per week in this study course so you can focus, set goals, and discover what God has to say about each area through the scriptures. In doing so, you will further develop for yourself the mind of Christ and begin speaking over your life in a way that delivers Your Kingdom Inheritance.

YKI also stands for *You Know It*. Each person knows within themselves the answers for what they need and where God is leading them.

"For example, whenever people who don't possess the law as their birthright commit sin, it still confirms that a "law" is present in their conscience. For when they instinctively do what the law requires, that becomes a "law" to govern them, even though they don't have Mosaic law. It demonstrates that the requirements of the law are woven into their hearts. They know what is right and wrong, for their conscience validates this "law" in their heart. Their thoughts correct them in one instance and commend them in another."
Romans 2:14–15 (TPT)

As a Christian, you are even more discerning because God has given you His Holy Spirit who lives inside of you. Through Him, you know the answers; they reside within you. Throughout this course, you will learn how to recognize those answers and walk in them through the power of the Holy Spirit, further transforming your life into the Lord's image day by day.

The Time You Invest Will Produce Valuable Results

Use this precious opportunity in class or personal study and set aside time each day to work on the homework and memorize scripture so you can truly transform your mind, which will transform your life. As you dedicate yourself to do this daily work, you will reap the benefits for yourself, and you will also be of greater value to God's kingdom. You will gain a stronger, more vibrant connection to God Himself— becoming more like Him with godly maturity and the power of the Holy Spirit!

From this place of spiritual growth, you will be better positioned to achieve your personal goals and gain a clearer understanding of the purpose of your success. You will gain relational wisdom and compassion for others as you dive deeper into God's truths, with the Holy Spirit guiding you.

Keep in mind, there is always a cost involved in achieving growth. As you sacrifice your time and dedicate yourself to new spiritual habits, you will reap a lifetime of benefits. Your intimate time with the Lord will cause you to grow in your faith, power, authority, and effectiveness. This continual connection with God empowers us to be productive for His kingdom. All honor, glory, and praise to Jesus for refining us for His glory!

Finding Freedom in a Broken World

God desires to heal us and give us complete restoration in all the things that concern us, which means He has something to say in His Word about each area of our life. It is therefore in our best interest to pay attention to His instructions. The more you listen to Him, the more He will speak, directing you in the way you should go. As you learn to recognize His voice and respond, it will bring you further victory by the power of the Holy Spirit. He will reveal to you how to overcome everything, just as He has overcome this world.

You have lived for quite some time by now in this broken, impure world which requires daily purification, or reprogramming with God. The Holy Spirit faithfully comes alongside us to guide and empower us so we can be transformed from our old patterns of thinking and behavior into the image and likeness of Christ.

We learn how to listen to the Holy Spirit by asking Him to search our heart and reveal broken areas; this ongoing process of active listening and being open to God's truth purifies us and restores us to our true self—the confident, powerful, successful self that God created every person to have. What is brought to the light gets healed!

This is what we are doing as we use Psalm 139:23–24 (TPT) as our guide:

"God, I invite Your searching gaze into my heart. Examine me through and through; find out everything that may be hidden within me. Put me to the test and sift through all my anxious cares. See if there is any path of pain I'm walking on, and lead me back to Your glorious, everlasting way— the path that brings me back to You."

This prayerful scripture means that you can bring your brokenness to Him, your perversions, your sins, your fears, your doubts, your concerns. Anything you want to know more about and be healed of, place that word into Psalm 139:23–24 to personalize the verse even more, and then bring it to God in faith and prayer. He will reveal the truth and healing that you need! Most people, Christians included, never spend time listening to God. They do a lot of talking sometimes, but not enough listening. Yet God is the most important person in the Universe! He created everything. He knows everything about you and how you are designed. He knows the plans He has for you, and they are good. Trust Him! He will heal you and lead you to life everlasting in the most glorious, beautiful, peaceful place you can imagine.

This process is up to you, and when you engage in it, you will benefit. So, allow God to continue to improve your life! There is always room for growth. When you think you have it all together and walk in pride, thinking you don't need to spend time learning and listening to God, that is when the enemy has great opportunity over your life, and he will creep in and destroy it. Even if it is little by little, that destruction will happen because the door has been opened, thus allowing him entrance into your life. You may not recognize it as it happens, because Satan is subtle, but his desire and every moment's goal is to destroy you.

Don't go that route! Humble yourself and seek God. Walk in His incredible power with the help of the Holy Spirit! God desires to bless you, and He will do so as you seek Him and walk in the maturity and direction of His way. Allow Him to take you from glory to glory and allow Him to continue to refine your life. It will be well worth it.

Jesus: The True Lord of Your Life

Let me pause for a moment and ask you if you have fully made Jesus the Lord of your life. Inviting Him in as Lord means that you trust Him to be the manager, the one in charge of every area of your life. When you accept Him, He will take up residence inside of you and begin to transform your life. You will hear His voice more clearly because He lives within you. He desires to live through you and to empower you in all you do!

Are you ready to accept Him? Doing so means you will have access to all wisdom, all strength, and all power through Him. Are you ready? If you have said yes, congratulations! You have just made the best decision of your life! Get ready to live an adventurous life filled with love and power!

There is something you need to also know about accepting Jesus as your Savior and Lord. The moment you accepted Him, you were given a call on your life to be His disciple here on earth. You became an instant evangelist! The Good News of the Gospel was never meant for you alone. God desires for you to share this Good News and help others come to know Him.

The most important way we do this is by example. You are to be His representative here on this earth! God desires to make known His presence inside of you to others. You hold great power within you because as a believer in Christ, you carry the Holy Spirit inside of you! Christ is in you!

He desires for you to do great things, and you are about to embark on that journey as you seek to improve every area of your life. Through this course of study, you are going to learn how to be incredibly successful for the benefit of others!

Remember and be encouraged by this: Our skills and our gifts were never meant to be for us alone. We are designed to be like God, who is very generous with all His impartations, so that we can both be blessed and be a blessing to the world.

Are you ready to allow God fully into your life so you can Be Transformed? Let's get started!

Week One

From Glory to Glory: Growing and Being Transformed into His Image

Have you ever looked at someone, compared their life to yours and wondered, "How is it that they are walking in success, while I am not? What is it that they know about success that is transforming their life? What am I missing that would help me to enjoy the accomplishments, rewards, and purpose that I see in others?"

Human beings tend to look at others who are being blessed and ask, "Why not me?" It's as though we sense, deep down, that there is another, better way we could be approaching our life. Fortunately, there truly is a more excellent way for us to follow—one that brings us into greater success, fulfillment, and joy.

I'm talking about God's way of living, which is available to all who have invited Jesus into their lives as Lord and Savior. Simply put, the answer to these questions about living a life filled with godly success is rooted in obeying the principles set forth in God's Word. When we seek to follow His will and line ourselves up with dedication to God in every area of life, that's when we are blessed as He intends. That's when our lives are transformed, receiving the favor and the fulfillment we long for.

The purpose of this book is to equip you to be *intentional* about this process of being transformed into His image, so you can create a life that honors God, which in turn provides a life filled with faith, joy, peace, confidence, and purpose. This is a life that brings God's kingdom to earth the way that it is in heaven—a life that God desires for you, His child, to have.

This transformation process begins with our thinking. As Proverbs 23:7 (TPT) reminds us, *"For as he thinks within himself, so is he."* Our thoughts are firmly intertwined with who we are—and who we can become. Our thoughts are powerful, and they can determine the directions we take.

In other words, the key difference between someone who is being successful and someone who is not experiencing success at a given time is the way they are *thinking*. God has so much to say about transforming our thoughts—so we can transform our lives! Instead of sabotaging our own lives, we can partner with God, becoming more like Him with our heavenly thoughts. When we think correctly, renewing our mind to think like Christ, we can begin to experience the triumph He has designed for us.

Change your mind, and you change your life!

A Mind that Thinks like God Thinks

Imagine having a mind that speaks positive, encouraging, faith-filled thoughts to you as you go about your daily activities. Imagine having an inner narration that says to you: "You're amazing! I love you! You can do anything you set yourself to achieve!" Wouldn't that make it so much more pleasant, positive, and exciting to live your life? Imagine how much more you could accomplish if what you say to yourself is the same as what God says is true about you!

This positive, godly self-talk is so important because our thinking is the key to our future. What we think determines what we believe, do, and receive in life. Yet we must renew our minds, according to God's Word.

We have all experienced things that have impacted how we see ourselves and how we think. We are surrounded by ideas that can discourage us from reaching our full potential. We may have gone through situations that have caused us to think poorly about ourselves. Perhaps we have found ourselves in circumstances that have led us to make choices that are not in harmony with God's best desires for our lives. Or we have come from dysfunctional families that distorted our understanding of what is normal and good. No one in our world is immune to having faulty thought patterns and habitual behaviors that hold us back from enjoying God's best for our lives.

In this broken world, there are offenses that may come, and things do shift and change in our life, but there is good news for the Christian. God has overcome the world and its brokenness! Seeking God to transform our life is to be under His management, as we call Jesus our Lord. When He is Lord, He will work for the good in our lives, and we can cooperate with the work He is doing. That is how transformation happens.

In this book, we are focused on the truth that comes from God Himself about who we are and what we are capable of. He is the one who has created us. We are loved by Him. He has called us overcomers, victorious through Him. We are fearfully and wonderfully made in His image. Having an inner godly voice that tells us we are powerful and capable of accomplishing our dreams and goals is what makes the difference in one's life. That is what this book is going to teach you how to do!

True, godly positive thinking is about aligning ourselves with what He says about who we are in Him. And God has given us the tools to take control of our thoughts. For this reason, God has instructed us to renew our minds, so we can be transformed.

In other words, you are not stuck where you are right now. You can change your life. You can discover the greater freedom, deliverance and joy God has for you.

As Christians, we always have potential to become more like Christ and more like our true selves in Him. To seek God is to be on the move, looking for more and more areas of our lives where we can be more like He is, being blessed and being a blessing to others. Living for Christ is the process of finding out what He is up to, and where He wants us to grow, where He wants to bring us in our life—which can bring great blessings to us and others.

Vision is so valuable in helping us accomplish our goals and be our best selves. True, godly vision is more than just a snapshot of your future. It is bigger than that! It is expansive and detail-oriented, showing you clearly where you want to be in every area of your life. Transforming ourselves into the image and likeness of Christ makes it possible to achieve the vision God has given to you for your life!

For this reason, we should always be wanting more—more of God, and more of His power and transformation in our life. Through His work in us, we are changed from glory to glory. Think about that for a moment—He is taking us from one good thing to the next good thing. The only way to be truly transformed is to seek new heights.

This means setting new goals and finding the purpose behind those goals so we can achieve them and continue growing. We are called to move upward and forward, to not stay complacent. It is all too easy to stay in our comfort zones, even if they are unhealthy. This is not of God. We are to be improving ourselves constantly, and we are called to help others improve theirs. As we enjoy God's best for ourselves, we can truly bless and influence others for good.

The Power of the Holy Spirit to Change Your Life

The concept of changing how we think may sound at first like the secular positive thinking techniques that the world often promotes. But the idea of choosing and taking our thoughts captive comes from God Himself. And as Christians, we have a key difference that is essential to our success, something that secular techniques don't have. That difference is the Holy Spirit, who is continually at work within us to bring us ever closer to God and His perfect will for our lives!

Jesus has said, *"I am the vine, you are the branches. He who abides in Me, and I in him, bears much fruit; for without Me you can do nothing"* (John 15:5 NKJV). Or as The Passion Translation expresses it, *"I am the sprouting vine and you're my branches. As you live in union with me as your source, fruitfulness will stream from within you—but when you live separated from me you are powerless."* No matter what the world may say, secular techniques can only take us so far. It is only when we draw on the Holy Spirit that we transform in the miraculous, life-changing way God intends.

When we live for Christ, the Holy Spirit dwells inside of us. He is in us, and we can draw from that power within to do what would be impossible for us to do in our own natural strength. We can begin to draw from His wisdom as we make decisions for our lives. We can draw on His boldness and courage when we are preparing to take action that would otherwise feel intimidating—whether it is the boldness to tell someone about Jesus, or the courage to apply for a new or better job, or the fearlessness we need to take a course in financial skills that will benefit us.

No matter what we are seeking to accomplish, the Holy Spirit brings God's divine, creative, dynamic power to the situation. As we learn to see life from His perspective, through the Word of God, and line up our lives to align with His Word and His will, we can operate from the place of strength, creativity, courage and faith that He desires for us.

Evaluation

The Central Scripture for This Course

"God, I invite your searching gaze into my heart.
Examine me through and through;
find out everything that may be hidden within me.
Put me to the test and sift through all my anxious cares.
See if there is any path of pain I'm walking on,
and lead me back to your glorious, everlasting way—
the path that brings me back to you."
Psalm 139:23–24 (TPT)

NIV
~~offensive~~
~~offsive~~
offensive

This is such an impactful scripture—one that emphasizes how we can gain greater awareness of our own heart and mind so we can invite God in and experience His transformational power. Let's break the scripture down so you can see how it will apply to your transformation over these seven weeks and beyond.

Search Me: Gaining Awareness

As we invite God to search us, we are being open to what He will show us, including where we may be sinning. We are also asking Him to "see" if we are walking on a path that is going to bring pain. Seeing is awareness, which is key to our being transformed and achieving the success we desire.

Being aware is the key to transformation. To begin the process of transformation, we first must become more aware of our lives by inviting God in to examine us. Remember, God desires to bless us richly in all the areas of life.

But we also have an enemy who wants to prevent us from becoming more like the Lord, more successful, more able to be a blessing as God intends. God says that we are to be aware because our enemy, the devil, comes as a roaring lion seeking whom he may devour (1 Peter 5:8). He is looking for opportunities to steal, kill and destroy—for ways to take us down and impede our progress. He will use anything he can to stop us—everyday things like rejection, or being misunderstood, or mistakes we make.

As we come to know the truth, what we discover can begin to set us free. Be honest with Him during this process and trust Him. Remember, He already knows the truth anyway, so nothing that is revealed will cause Him to love you any less.

When we are honest with the Lord and with ourselves, we remove the pride that gets in the way of true transformation. He has your good in mind, and He will bring about good through this process as you cooperate with Him.

Throughout this seven-week journey, you will be learning how to listen to the voice of God, allowing Him to show you where your broken thoughts are so He can give you the correct, godly thoughts to think about. Find out where the pain is at in your life, so together with God, you can heal it. What are your fears? Doubts? Concerns? Goals? Dreams? Passions? Bring it all to Him and allow Him to begin to speak to you about it. He will not let you down.

Remember, it's how we think about our careers, relationships, wealth and health that determines what we have. God desires you to be successful in each and every area of your life. And the key to right thinking begins with awareness—a concept that God gave us to empower us.

Know My Heart: Identifying Your Belief System

Our heart is our belief system, and what we believe becomes evident in our habits and our thinking. "Know my heart" means knowing the truth about yourself in a given situation. Transformation begins with the truth, which is the number one thing we require to grow and be changed. God says that when we know the truth, it will set us free. *"For if you embrace the truth, it will release true freedom into your lives"* (John 8:32 TPT).

Everything in this course is based on knowing the truth. As we ask God to search our heart, we can discover what is true about how we are functioning in our relationships, our work, our wellness, and our spiritual life. As we see more clearly what is in our heart—what we think and believe—it allows us to make the godly changes necessary to benefit us and bless us.

Everything depends on our heart and our belief system. To be transformed, we must align our heart with our mind. God desires to give us a new belief system, one that equips us to trust in and believe in Him, and surrender to His ways, allowing Him to transform our mind and our life. That's the new heart He can give us.

As I coach my clients, often they say to me, "I know these things… But they're not in my heart." That's where the tools in this course become useful. They are designed to help you align your heart and mind, so you can achieve congruency, or agreement, between them. As you learn to believe that God has given you a new heart, you will take thoughts captive and make them obedient to your beliefs and transfer them from your mind back into your heart, so they can then become authentically you. And then, out of your heart will come the truth that is good and beautiful, living in and working through you.

Test Me: Recognizing Areas for Growth

We find out where we are lacking—and where we are successful—when we are tested. Perhaps you have a busy day with your children, and you feel yourself becoming impatient. This reveals where you have a lack; you need more patience. When we're tested in our relationships, we find out if our love for that person is truly there. When we're tested about anxiety, it uncovers where we can grow in faith and trust in the Lord.

It's this way with every test we face. The situation and our response to it shows what we are in need of. And this sets us into a position where we can know the truth and be set free to grow more like Christ. We memorize scriptures throughout the seven weeks of this course to help us know the truth and be able to apply it when we are tested, so that our growth can be based in what God says about us.

Anxious Thoughts, Offensive Ways: Growing More Like God

As we pray and allow the Lord to search our heart and reveal truth to us, we can change these words in the scriptures we're memorizing (especially Psalm 139) to address whatever may concern us. He can search us to see if there are any lazy ways within us, or any stubborn ways, or sinful ways, or rude ways, or fearful ways.

Imagine the transformations that become possible as we ask the Lord to search us and show us what is causing us to be unsuccessful in an area. This is where you will begin to grow, because as you ask Him to search you, He can come in and work within you. This is where His sanctification takes place and growth begins to happen.

As we face such situations, we can ask the Lord to show us if there is anything we are doing that is not productive or godly, and to make us aware of what is true so that we can grow.

Sometimes, the situation is not our issue, but someone else's. God can show us what is true—about the other individual, or about us and how we can grow. No matter what, He can reveal to us what we can do to be more like Him.

For example, I am someone who grew up in a dysfunctional home. When I sense that I am facing a challenge in a relationship, I go to the Lord and ask Him to search me, to see if there is anything I can do differently. I ask Him to show me how I can continue to rise above the things that have happened in my life. As I ask Him to search me and know my heart, layer by layer He can begin to work in me, transforming me, and freeing me so that I can be a leader in my sphere of influence.

God took my hurts and healed them and gave me the mind of Christ, so I wouldn't have a lack. Still, as life happens day by day, I go to Him knowing there is always a need He will fulfill.

One of the needs I had was that of a mother's approval and favor. He continually fills that need. Where I need comfort, He offers it to me; where I need wisdom, He gives that to me. I continually ask Him to search me and to work within me. Because of that, I am able to be free of my lack, becoming filled so I can be there for my children. I am free to be their comfort, their encouragement, showing them love and celebrating their accomplishments. I am not hindered by a wounded heart, and I can now love my children and grandchildren in the way I longed to be loved myself as a daughter.

And through transformations like this in my own life, I have seen how powerful it is when we invite God into our lives. I've seen how aligning our mind and our heart equips us with a belief system that brings true and lasting, godly transformations. And I want the same for you.

Life isn't always easy. There are days when someone doesn't give us the kudos we need, or something goes wrong that trips us up. On those days, we can use the tools in this course to remind ourselves what God says and refocus our minds and draw upon our belief system in Him so that we can be free.

Inviting God into Every Area of Our Life

To bring the truth to the forefront in our lives, we use what I refer to in my coaching ministry as the Circle of Personal Perspective (the Circle)—pictured below. In this course, you will use this concept as you examine these six key areas of your life.

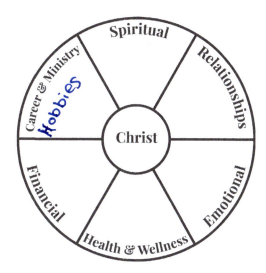

As you look at the Circle above, you can see that for a Christian, the center of the Circle—and the center of our life—is Christ Himself. He is at the core of who we are and what we do. Expanding outward from that point are the various areas of life—our spirituality, relationships, emotional wellness, physical health, finances, and career as well as ministry, which is simply any way in which you serve others.

Each area of the Circle has its own unique aspects, which can change from day to day as our lives shift and change. Some days, we may feel emotionally fantastic, for example, while other days we may feel down or sapped of mental strength.

Notice, too, that the areas of the Circle are connected, which means that what is happening in one area can affect others. If we are financially struggling, it may cause us to feel emotionally discouraged. If our relationships are under stress, we may find ourselves eating poorly. For this reason, being aware of how we are doing in each area of the Circle on a daily or weekly basis is helpful to us as we grow in the Lord. This honest self-awareness gives us the information we need to recognize what is happening in our lives, so we can make adjustments that are good for us.

Seek Balance in All Areas of Life

What is amazing about living with Christ in the center of our life is that His truth, love and guidance can benefit all six areas of our personal Circle. As you improve one area through His help, it will improve so many other areas of your life as well.

The Circle is therefore a vivid reminder that in His love for us, God sees us as whole and balanced in every way. He has something to say about each area of our life, and when we line up our lives with His will, we are blessed, and we enjoy a healthy balance, rest, encouragement, and growth.

Receiving His blessing is a lot like the law of gravity—what goes up must come down. As we align ourselves with His will, the natural results of obeying Him and pleasing Him are bound to follow. We see this concept play out in every area. If we work hard and do our job to our employer's satisfaction, we receive our paycheck—and maybe even a promotion in due time. As we act kindly toward others, we receive more opportunities for kindness and love in return.

This concept of action and reaction, of sowing and receiving, does not mean that you are not loved already, just as you are. You cannot remove God's love for you (Romans 8:38). What it does mean is that we are seeking to love and honor God by obeying Him, and in turn He is able to bless us in greater measure because He is true to His Word.

We can use the Circle and self-examination throughout our lives to create pathways to greater and greater growth. It provides a strong foundation for knowing where we are at and deciding where we want to go next. It gives insight into the key areas of life, showing us what needs attention so that we can gain balance. We can then align ourselves better with God's will and that which is good in our lives, which equips us to live life as God intends.

The Circle is also an excellent tool for helping you to guide your family members, friends, and others into their purpose and goals. As you come to appreciate its value and learn how to use it, it can serve as a great way to open up communication with those around you and provide support and encouragement that can help them move forward in life as well.

The 5 Keys to Success

As we continue through the next six weeks of activities, we will make use of several tools and techniques that can help you in your process of being transformed. The first is a life-changing concept I use in my YKI coaching ministry—"The 5 Keys to Success." This is the tool you will use as you apply what you discover through the weekly self-evaluations that lead you on your journey of growth and transformation into the image of Christ.

The five keys will help you as you move from the place where you are at right now—which is often a place you wish to change or grow in—to a place where you will enjoy a fulfilled, joyful, successful life in the Lord. These keys can be applied to any area of life and any issue you are facing, equipping you to make good decisions and take actions that will lead you to success.

You'll use these keys over the next seven weeks as you begin the transformation process.

Key 1: Truth

God said you shall know the ***truth***, and the truth will set you free (John 8:32). Many people think of this scripture as talking specifically about religion, but it is so much more than that. It applies to every area of life. Knowing the truth about ourselves is like putting a dot on the map and seeing where we are at. It will be difficult to move forward if you don't know first where you are at on the map of your life right now.

So, you can see how important it is to God—and to us—to know ourselves and understand what is true about our situations. What is the truth about how we communicate? What is true about how we're serving others? What is the truth about others? What is true about our emotional wellness? Are we taking the steps we need to take to care for ourselves properly? How do we think about money—and is our thinking true? What is true about our career?

When we know these answers to questions like these, we can make better choices for ourselves. Becoming aware of what is true can create opportunities for greater growth and more freedom.

Each week, you will consider the truth about the area you are working on. You'll ask yourself honestly what the truth is about where you are at in each area right now. Beginning with the truth will help you discover where you'd like to be, so you can begin to move in the direction you'd like to go.

Key 2: Goal and Purpose

After you gain clarity on where you are and where you want to be, you can begin to set clear goals. If the truth is like marking your life map with where you are right now, then your goal is like marking the map with your desired destination.

Knowing your *goals* will make it easier to move toward them with focus and boldness, so you can accomplish the *purposes* God has for your life. And it's important to look for the purpose behind any goal you want to achieve, because this is what helps us to be persistent in moving forward. For example, as you consider your spirituality, you might decide you would like to focus more on God's Word daily through prayer or Bible study.

As you consider your purpose for that goal, you'll gain the motivation that will encourage you to pursue your goal with passion and enthusiasm. You may decide that for you, the purpose of knowing more of God's Word is that it will help you walk in peace and confidence, making you more effective in all that you do. And that purpose will inspire you to reach your goal.

Key 3: Plan

God says that if we are going to build a house, we must first plan it out (Luke 14:28–30). After you have set goals and become clear on your purpose for achieving them, you can begin to develop your *plan* for how you will accomplish your goals.

You might think of this process as being similar to planning a road trip. You've marked your map with where you are right now (point A—the truth), and you've marked your destination (point B—your goal). You've identified the reason for your trip (your purpose). Now, you can figure out the road that will take you to your destination. That's your plan—a specific set of actions that will take you from point A to point B.

As you create plans for the goals you set in this course, you'll be able to turn your idea or desire into something that is tangible. For example, if your goal is to establish a better relationship with your spouse so you can experience more peace and joy (your purpose), then your plan might be to compliment your spouse daily as well as performing one act of service for them each day.

Key 4: Action and Accountability

Once your plan is made, you will take **action** to fulfill it. You'll identify and develop clear action steps that are straightforward and doable. Remember, it's not enough to set goals and make a plan. There must be action, because it is in action—in doing—that your goals and plans begin to take shape so you can create the life you desire.

To help yourself take the actions that will get you to success, it's important to find **accountability partners**—people of like faith who are trustworthy and will encourage you to keep moving toward your good and godly goals.

As you remain firm in your own goals, purposes, and plans, you can expect to find some resistance from others—but there will also be people who cheer you on. Make room for these cheerleaders in your life. They will help you feel energized to keep going until you reach your desired destination.

Simply notice who supports you in your journey and who doesn't. For anyone who is not providing accountability and support, you can politely set boundaries that work for you so that you can keep moving forward. Greet them kindly but be prepared to gently move on about your business.

Remember, you must follow through with your plans to experience a transformed life. Without follow-through, your goals are only dreams. Action and trusted accountability partners help you turn those dreams into reality.

[handwritten note: giving back = blessing]

Key 5: Success

Finally, as you accomplish your goals, it is time to celebrate your accomplishments. When you follow these keys, there is no way you won't be successful—because God is in it, leading you and telling you how to be successful. When you do what He says, you will be a success! You will achieve your goals and rise above the challenges you once faced.

God is faithful, and He will help you to follow through with your plans! The rewards of pursuing goals that line up with His desires will begin to pour into your life. This is the point where the 5 Keys to Success then must be repeated, daily, so you can continue to grow in Him. And it is also the point when you can give back and bless others as you have been blessed—which is also God's desire for you, as it gives your life purpose and meaning as well as furthers His Kingdom.

We are designed to give back. If we are not willing to give back, we may find it hard to achieve the success we want, because we are not following His design for us.

As you enjoy the rewards of a transformed life, you can then begin to ask new questions about where to go next: "What purpose can I move into now that I am blessed? Who will I help? What plan of action will I take to bless others?" Proverbs 11:25 in the *Message* translation tells us, "*The one who blesses others is abundantly blessed; those who help others are helped.*" This verse in *The Passion Translation* says, "*Those who live to bless others will have blessings heaped upon them, and the one who pours out his life to pour out blessings will be saturated with favor.*" When we receive success and pass it on, it perpetuates our success.

This is the whole reason we do what we do as Christians. We were designed to give back, which gives us a greater purpose! Once we achieve our goals, we can rejoice in what we have, glorify Him, and share the good news with others of how God can bless them as He blessed us.

The "I AM" Rule

The phrase "I AM" means God. In Exodus 3:14, God tells Moses, *"I AM who I AM."* He is called the "Great I AM." And throughout Scripture, He declares who He is using "I AM" statements.

God is the great I AM, and we are created by God in His beautiful image. *"So God created man and woman and shaped them with His image inside of them. In his own **beautiful** image, he created his **masterpiece**"* (Genesis 1:27 TPT). He created us as a masterpiece and to be like Him. In addition, Deuteronomy 31:8 (NIV) says, *"The Lord himself goes before you and will be with you; he will never leave you nor forsake you. Do not be afraid; do not be discouraged."* Because God is the great I AM, we could say this as, "The great I AM Himself goes before us."

Since we are created in God's image and He promises to go before us, we can use I AM statements to encourage ourselves and invite Him to go before us in every area of life—so that we can follow Him into greater success.

The I AM rule is a tool for knowing and speaking out who we are in Christ. As He is, so are we in this world. As we identify and seek to live out who we are in Christ, we become more like Him. We align those qualities in our heart and mind by speaking them out, confessing them, praying them and meditating on them.

It is so essential to speak only what He says is true about ourselves. What does that mean? It means we use what the Bible says as we anchor ourselves in our true identity in Christ. It means speaking to ourselves like this:

"I AM victorious. I AM a son or daughter of the King. I AM an ambassador for Christ on the Earth. I AM representing the Lord. I AM kind. I am loving. I AM flexible. I AM faithful. I AM equipped."

At first glance, this may seem similar to the secular concepts of affirmations and positivity. And these are good things. But as Christians, we base our positive statements in the powerful, godly knowledge of who we are in Christ. Our affirmations and positive beliefs are rooted and grounded in God and His Word, which is a sure foundation for us to build our lives upon. And with the Holy Spirit empowering us to live according to God's Word, we have His power to draw upon in living out the I AM statements we are making.

The I AM tool can be particularly effective when we are faced with difficult situations that can provoke us into bad thought patterns or old habitual ways of thinking and behaving that do not align with God's will for our life. The I AM rule is a tool to help us transform these habitual thinking patterns and behaviors from what is negative to what is positive and godly.

For example, we may experience a moment at the grocery store which causes frustration or anger. Using the I AM rule doesn't mean being dishonest about our life or how we are feeling. But it means being precise with our words and acknowledging the difference between what is true and eternal, versus what is temporary and subject to change, such as our feelings, which change all the time.

Use "I feel" to address the things that are temporary and subject to change in your life. "I am feeling angry and sad right now" is a lot different than saying, "I am angry and sad." One is temporary, while the other sounds permanent. Our mind knows the difference. We use the I AM rule to build on what our mind already knows and accepts; we additionally speak what is true about how God sees us.

Godly Anchoring

In our practice, we use the sense of smell to further anchor into our minds our true identity and power. Let me explain:

Have you ever walked past a bakery, smelled some cookies, and said, "That takes me right back to time with Grandma?" Or perhaps you've smelled a particular flower, and it brought you back in your mind to a time that flower was meaningful to you, such as your first date.

This happens because the mind and the senses work together. They are designed to do so. And we can use this to our benefit.

We all have a God-given ability to use our five senses to prepare ourselves for success. Godly anchoring is a technique that empowers us to do so. In godly anchoring, we learn to connect something we experience with our senses (in this course, we choose a delightful scent placed in the palms of our hands, which I'll explain below) to a positive feeling or thought we desire to have. This linking of scent and positive I AM statements is an effective tool that moves us out of negative thoughts and behavior patterns we wish to change, so we can move toward the goals we have.

Much like a boat that throws down an anchor to keep itself in the proper location, godly anchoring is a method of turning our thoughts to what is positive and true. It allows us to stay rooted in that thought, bringing congruency between our mind and our heart. And godly anchoring is a technique that we can easily use anywhere, anytime, as we need it.

The first step to creating a godly anchor for yourself is to choose a positive biblical thought based on our identity in Christ—such as "I AM blessed, protected, capable and successful." This is the thought that you will link to the sensory input of the essential oil being placed in your palms.

Remember, these "I AM" statements are based on who God says we are, and because they come from God, they are powerful for changing us into His image and producing joy and peace inside us! When you use the words, "I AM," make sure to anchor and identify yourself to Him and to use only the words that confirm who God says you are!

You can choose your anchoring I AM statements according to what would be most beneficial to you at any given time. For example, if you are preparing to seek a job, your I AM statement might be, "I AM blessed and highly favored of God, and He blesses all I set my hands to accomplish." When you go to a job interview, you can use the act of godly anchoring, with your chosen essential oil placed in the palms of your hands, to help you concentrate on the I AM statement and be focused on what is positive and true about you in Christ.

I encourage you to use the palms of your hands as your anchor, along with a pleasant essential oil, as a reminder of our Savior Jesus, whose death and resurrection paved the way for all our blessings. Use godly anchoring as an opportunity to remember who Christ is, and how He has taken everything upon Himself so that we might be free and forgiven in Him.

Godly Meditation and Visualization

People achieve what they desire when they experience it in their mind. What we imagine and envision, we can accomplish.

An example I like to give is to think of a baby on the verge of learning to walk. The baby sees others walking—parents, siblings, friends—and studies what they do so they can learn to walk. They imagine that they can do it, and then they start doing it until they are good at it. The baby, in other words, visualizes the possibility of walking before actually achieving it.

Likewise, we can create imagery in our minds for anything we desire to achieve. We can first see ourselves doing it, and then move forward into action. For example, we might see ourselves walking confidently into our next job interview. We can use godly anchoring and I AM statements to remind us of what is true about us in Christ, and then we can visualize ourselves having a calm, productive conversation with our interviewer—articulately offering great answers, sharing our thoughts, listening carefully, asking great questions, and showing our enthusiasm for the job. The more we visualize this, the easier it will be to do it, because in our mind we will already have experienced it. It will be real to us.

Visualization is that powerful!

The wisdom of using meditation, contemplation, and visualization to renew our minds and adopt healthy thinking patterns is from God! He gave us our minds and told us to use them for His glory and our benefit. It is very biblical to use our mind, vision, and imagination for God's glory.

As long as what we envision lines up with His Word, the results will be powerful and positive. God wants us to think about that which is lovely and of good report. As we focus on what is good, these things grow in our minds and become our realities. Our lives become aligned with the good that God intended.

To not have vision is to be hopeless. (See Proverbs 29:18.) But God offers hope! He desires us to envision all that will be ours, based on the Bible's promises.

Perhaps you are in need of healing. Begin to see yourself receiving your healing and walking in health and wholeness. Picture yourself healed and engaged in all the daily activities of a healed person. Or perhaps you may need emotional wellness. Visualize yourself filled with joy and peace in the Lord!

As you use your creative abilities to picture yourself walking in the fullness of all God has for you, you will begin to transform your thought patterns so they can align with the Bible's promises and begin to experience them coming to pass for you.

Daily Questions to Guide You in Your Self-Evaluation

There are so many possibilities and opportunities that can stimulate our minds as we take time to see what is true about our lives right now and decide where we would like to go from here. To aid you in this growth process, this course provides you with daily homework to accelerate your growth, as well as a daily scripture to meditate upon and memorize.

As you answer these questions honestly, you'll begin to see where you are at in each area of life. And this truth will make it possible to begin the transformation process. Ask God to search you and show you the answers. Set aside the time you are going to do this each day and spend at least 15–20 minutes getting closer to God and allowing Him to reveal hidden secrets to you.

As you engage in this self-evaluation process, I want to encourage you that this is simply a tool to help you to check in with yourself and the Lord daily, so you may search yourself according to the wisdom of Psalm 139. Remember that God loves you and values you exactly where you are at right now, and there is no condemnation for those who are in Christ (Romans 8:1). He loves you no matter where you've been, what you've done, what's been done to you—God loves you in an immeasurable amount that is beyond comprehension.

God also wants the best for you. He desires for you to grow and be more like Him. As you learn to check in and recognize where you are at daily, you will begin to see areas in your life where you would like to see God's power at work to transform you. This is such an exciting and worthwhile process!

I also encourage you to remember that there are no strict rules to follow about answering the questions. You are free to decide the best way for yourself to check in, and you may answer the questions in the way that serves you best.

If you prefer to write thoughtful answers and reflect on them, it is perfectly acceptable to do so. For those who can appreciate the idea of assessing yourself with a number from 1 to 10 in each area or question, you are welcome to do so. In the Appendix, you will find an explanation on how to do so and a longer list of questions to offer you for your self-evaluation.

The key is to choose a method of engaging with the questions that is comfortable and inspiring to you, and then to do it daily throughout this course so that your consistent check-ins can provide opportunities for self-understanding and growth. In doing so, you can discover your current truth and see more clearly the areas where God is encouraging you to be more like Him.

Remember that God desires every area of your life to be as great as it can be. You can assess even the little things you do that add up to great value—such as getting outside for fresh air and exercise, making good choices with your eating habits, and drinking enough water. Making adjustments, even when they appear small, will bring you so much benefit as you make time to be aware of what you need. Awareness is such a gift that God has made available for us all and will take each of us from glory to glory. Your self-assessment is simply a way to use His gift to create more benefits for yourself throughout your life! Onward, glorious one!

Day 1: From Glory to Glory

Spirituality
Self-Discovery and Goals

Each day this week, consider the following scripture and how it applies to the area you are examining—which today is spirituality. Each day this week, I will add the daily topic in parenthesis into the scripture below, as a reminder to personalize Psalm 139 for each day's activities and prayers, inviting God into your life to help you grow, be healed, and be free.

> *"God, I invite your searching gaze into my heart.*
> *Examine me through and through;*
> *find out everything that may be hidden within me (regarding my spiritual life).*
> *Put me to the test and sift through all my anxious (spiritual) cares.*
> *See if there is any path of pain I'm walking on,*
> *and lead me back to your glorious, everlasting way—*
> *the path that brings me back to you."*
> **Psalm 139:23–24 (TPT)**

Take note that the answers to these questions simply reflect how you feel toward your spiritual life right now. God always loves you, and He never leaves you (Romans 8:38), so you can be free to be honest in how you answer these questions, without fear of His rejection. He desires us to search ourselves, for our own good. This is about you and your own growth, and your own desire to get closer to God.

Take a moment right now to think about your spiritual life. Where would you assess that you are right now? I encourage you to remember that simply by reading this book and pursuing something that is spiritually good for you, you are doing something positive for yourself in this area of life.

Here are some questions to help guide you as you consider your spiritual life.

1. What is the **truth** about where I am in my relationship with God?

   _____
   _____
   _____

2. What are my spiritual **goals** and their **purposes**?

3. How do I **plan** on getting there?

4. Who will help hold me **accountable** for my **action** steps?

5. When I become more connected to God, how will I **help others**?

Pray

Thank You, Lord, for helping me to gain a closer walk with You. Soften my heart and reveal to me any areas where my ways are not in line with Your will and Your Word. Show me where I can be more like You in all I do. Help me to get the right people in my life so I can remain close to You and help others.

Day 2

Relationships
Self-Discovery and Goals

*"God, I invite your searching gaze into my heart.
Examine me through and through;
find out everything that may be hidden within me (regarding my relationships).
Put me to the test and sift through all my anxious cares (in my relationships).
See if there is any path of pain I'm walking on,
and lead me back to your glorious, everlasting way—
the path that brings me back to you."*
Psalm 139:23–24 (TPT)

As you did for spirituality, now consider your relationships. You may want to give yourself an overall assessment that applies to your relationships in general, as well as considering a particular relationship that matters most to you right now.

For example, you might feel you are doing great with most people you know, but right now your connection with your spouse or child is in need of greater growth. It is ok to acknowledge this. Your goal right now is simply to gain information and be truthful with yourself, so that you can begin to set goals and make changes that are healthy and good for you. With that in mind, answer the following relationship questions.

1. What is the truth about where I am at in each of my relationships?

2. What are my relationship goals and their purposes?

3. How do I plan on getting there?

4. Who will help hold me accountable for my action steps?

5. When I achieve success in my relationships, how will I help others?

Pray

Help me, Lord, to discover the truth of all aspects in my relationships. Reveal to me areas in my life where I can grow in how I relate in healthy ways to others. Help my relationship choices to be pleasing to You and filled with purpose for Your glory, Lord.

Week One: From Glory to Glory: Growing and Being Transformed into His Image

Day 3

Emotional Wellness
Self-Discovery and Goals

*"God, I invite your searching gaze into my heart.
Examine me through and through;
find out everything that may be hidden within me (regarding my emotional life).
Put me to the test and sift through all my anxious (emotional) cares.
See if there is any path of pain I'm walking on,
and lead me back to your glorious, everlasting way—
the path that brings me back to you."*
Psalm 139:23–24 (TPT)

Now, consider your emotional wellness—which can include such things as how you care for your emotions, what you do to manage your emotions, and how emotionally balanced you may feel. You may want to give yourself an assessment that applies to your emotions in general, as well as considering particular situations in which you know your emotions are strong, or where you may feel challenged in your emotional life.

For example, you might feel that in general, your emotional wellness is very healthy right now, but on the job or in your marriage, you may feel like you are not as emotionally balanced as you'd like to be. It is good to take note of important areas and circumstances in your life that are in need of changes, so that you can be emotionally well as God intends. With that in mind, consider the following emotional wellness questions.

1. What is the truth about where I am at in my emotional health?

   _____
   _____
   _____

2. What are my goals and their purposes for my emotional health?

   _____
   _____
   _____

3. How do I plan on getting there?

4. Who will help hold me accountable for my action steps?

5. When I achieve emotional wellness, how will I help others?

Pray

Help me, Lord, to discover more about my emotional health. Reveal to me areas where I may be making choices or holding onto beliefs that impede my emotional wellness. I want to live filled with your peace and joy so I can fulfill all that you have for me.

Day 4

Physical Wellness
Self-Discovery and Goals

*"God, I invite your searching gaze into my heart.
Examine me through and through;
find out everything that may be hidden within me (regarding my physical life).
Put me to the test and sift through all my anxious (physical) cares.
See if there is any path of pain I'm walking on,
and lead me back to your glorious, everlasting way—
the path that brings me back to you."*
Psalm 139:23–24 (TPT)

In this section, consider your physical well-being. You may want to give yourself an overall assessment that applies to your physical wellness in general, and then make note of any areas of your physical health that matter the most to you right now.

For example, you may consider yourself to be physically healthy with an acknowledgement to yourself about the healthy eating habits you have established. Or perhaps you have a health challenge that has you feeling physically down right now, and you wish to make some improvements. With that in mind, consider the following physical wellness questions.

1. What is the truth about where I am at in my physical health?

    _____
    _____
    _____

2. What are my goals and their purposes for my physical health?

    _____
    _____
    _____

3. How do I plan on getting there?

4. Who will help hold me accountable for my action steps?

5. When I achieve physical wellness, how will I help others?

Pray

Lord, thank You that You have created me in Your image. Help me to care for my body in ways that are pleasing to You. Equip me to make good choices that promote physical wellness so that I can feel good and healthy and also accomplish my goals and Your purpose for my life.

Day 5

Financial Wellness
Self-Discovery and Goals

*"God, I invite your searching gaze into my heart.
Examine me through and through;
find out everything that may be hidden within me (regarding my financial life).
Put me to the test and sift through all my anxious (financial) cares.
See if there is any path of pain I'm walking on, and lead me back to your glorious,
everlasting way—the path that brings me back to you."*
Psalm 139:23–24 (TPT)

As you consider the financial area of life, keep in mind that even when finances seem tight, there are many things you can do to prepare yourself for future success and growth. Perhaps you are taking classes in budgeting, or researching places to open a bank account, or considering ways in which you can earn more income. All these things factor into your financial condition.

1. What is the truth about where I am at financially right now?

   _____
   _____
   _____

2. What are my goals and their purposes for my finances?

   _____
   _____
   _____

3. How do I plan on getting there?

   _____
   _____
   _____

4. Who will help hold me accountable for my action steps?

5. When I achieve financial success, how will I give back?

Pray

Lord, thank You that You provide for me. Reveal to me any areas where I am holding onto doubts about Your desire to provide for my needs. Help me to manage my money well, so that what I do is pleasing to You. Help me to be successful in this area of my life.

Day 6

Career and Ministry
Self-Discovery and Goals

"God, I invite your searching gaze into my heart.
Examine me through and through;
find out everything that may be hidden within me (regarding career, ministry, serving others).
Put me to the test and sift through all my anxious (career, ministry, serving) cares.
See if there is any path of pain I'm walking on,
and lead me back to your glorious, everlasting way—
the path that brings me back to you."
Psalm 139:23-24 (TPT)

Now, it is time to consider the area of career and ministry (serving others). If there are different areas in which you work, such as having more than one job, or working for pay as well as some work you do at home, you may wish to assess each of these areas.

In addition, I realize that not everyone who reads this book has a desire to be a pastor or some other form of full-time ministry. This is perfectly ok. Remember that whatever we do for a living is a form of ministry as we are serving others in that role. Wherever you interact with others, that is form of serving and being a blessing. Take a moment to consider any volunteering or ministry you may do right now.

1. What is the truth about how I am doing in my career and ministry?

   _____
   _____
   _____

2. What are my goals and their purposes for my career and ministry?

   _____
   _____
   _____

3. How do I plan on getting there?

   _____
   _____
   _____

4. Who will help hold me accountable for my action steps?

   _____
   _____
   _____

5. When I achieve success in this area, how will I give back?

   _____
   _____
   _____

Pray

Lord, thank You that You have given me the ability to work and have purpose. Open my eyes to the good plans You have for me in the areas of my career, volunteer work, and ministry. Help me to walk in your desires and plans as I serve others. No matter what I do, Lord, help me to work as if I am working for You.

Day 7

Rest
Self-Discovery and Goals

*"God, I invite your searching gaze into my heart.
Examine me through and through;
find out everything that may be hidden within me (regarding rest).
Put me to the test and sift through all my anxious cares (related to rest).
See if there is any path of pain I'm walking on,
and lead me back to your glorious, everlasting way—
the path that brings me back to you."*
Psalm 139:23–24 (TPT)

Finally, it is time to enjoy a sabbath rest. Take a moment right now to think about the place that rest has in your life. Where would you assess that you are right now in the area of rest? It is so valuable to take time to reflect on your rest and to make time to be refreshed in your life. This aspect of living is important enough to God that He tells us to take one day each week in which to rest. After you prayerfully consider these questions, make time to relax and enjoy your day!

1. What is the truth about how I rest?

2. What are my goals and their purposes in the area of resting?

3. What plans can I set in place to rest in the context of what I do each day?

4. Who will help hold me accountable for my action steps?

5. When I am able to rest in the Lord, how will I help others do the same?

Pray

Lord, thank You that You have given me rest. I know that resting in You is what gives me great peace and contentment. Help me to rest even during the times that I must work.

Week One: From Glory to Glory: Growing and Being Transformed into His Image

Write Your Inner Narration

"Stop imitating the ideals and opinions of the culture around you but be inwardly transformed by the Holy Spirit through a total reformation of how you think. This will empower you to discern God's will as you live a beautiful life, satisfying and perfect in his eyes."
Romans 12:2 (TPT)

Each of us has an inner narrator—a voice inside our heads that reflects how we think about ourselves and how we talk to ourselves.

Remember that God's words are positive. His words lift and encourage you. What He says is the exact opposite of any negative thoughts and lies that you have been led to believe. There are tools in the Appendix that can help you discover positive, loving things God says are true about you—words you can learn to apply to your own life day by day to help you transform your thinking so that you see yourself and speak to yourself as the person God has made you to be — a confident, beloved, valuable person who has a great destiny from the Lord.

Faith comes by what we hear. *"Faith, then, is birthed in a heart that responds to God's anointed utterance of the Anointed One"* (Romans 10:17 TPT). As you get His Word deep into your innermost being, your heart and soul, His words begin to turn into reality in your life, empowering your transformation into His image.

As you answer the questions in each day's assignment section, take notice of any negative words you have written and transform them into the positive version of what God would say. Additionally, take notice of the positive words you have written down and include those in your godly narration. Keep building upon your godly narration each day so you can continue to transform into who you are in Christ.

Here is an example from my life to help you see how to apply this technique:

When I think about the first question on spirituality— "What is true about my relationship with the Lord?"—I would personally say that I commune with Him every day, because it keeps me connected with Him. I can take that word "connected," and put it in my narration for that day or that week:

"I AM connected with the Lord."

When I'm anchoring myself, I can speak those words over myself: "I AM connected with the Lord." It's meaningful and helpful to me.

You can follow the same approach. There are so many wonderful words that you can use as you speak life over yourself. The words that are of God are vast. You can find a list in my book *A Coach for Christ* that you can reference, as well as in the *Who I Am in Christ* section of the Appendix of this workbook.

Writing your new inner narration is all about using synonyms and antonyms. If the word you are drawn to is positive, you can use it and any words like it in your personal narration. If a word comes to mind that is negative, perhaps because it is something negative that has been spoken over you in the past, you can use its opposite.

For example, if you happened to answer the question about your relationship with God right now with something like, "I don't feel close to Him," you would speak the opposite over yourself in your narration. "I do feel close to Him. I AM connected with Him."

Follow this process with all the questions you answer in the activities this week, and throughout the remaining weeks of this class. Create a list of positive, life-giving, godly words for yourself on your narration sheet, and use them to create a written narration that you can speak over yourself as often as you like. (There are sample narrations at the end of each week's activities, as well as in the Appendix section, to give you inspiration as you create your own personalized version.)

Here is an example of a godly, encouraging, positive narration to get you started:

"I AM beautiful. I AM loved by God, just as I AM. I AM forgiven.
I AM pleasing to God. I AM strong. I AM courageous…"

Follow that pattern and additionally write something else below that fits with how God sees you and how you want to see yourself. Then read and say this narration out loud at least twice a day, morning and night. Read it over and over, especially when you are feeling discouraged. Speak it over yourself in the present tense and anchor yourself in Christ. These new, godly characteristics will begin to get into your heart and mind, and with each day, they will become more and more natural to think about yourself with an inner narration that is lined up with God's truth — which is the real you!

Week Two
Spirituality

The path to true, lasting change begins with our relationship with God. Coming to know the Lord is the most important decision we can ever make in our lives, and it is the foundation upon which all godly changes must be built. His power at work within us can bring about true, life-changing transformation in every area of our life.

We are meant to be in relationship with God. It's what we were created for! And God is the greatest life coach there is. So, it makes sense that as we achieve balance, renewal, and growth in the spiritual area of life, we will begin to see growth in other areas as well.

Our spirituality can empower us to make decisions that are good and godly. This is where we gain the will and the faith to take the steps we need to walk according to God's Word, standing on His promises in the Bible. It is where we gain the ability to be like Jesus. When Christians know their true identity in Christ, great things happen! Revival happens!

Spirituality, however, doesn't simply happen by chance. It is based on a living, evolving, ever-growing relationship with the Lord—one that we must nurture and make time for daily.

Jesus Our Savior

Everything begins with our connection with God. And we all need to be transformed! Remember, none of us are born righteous. We are born a sinner. Due to sin, we were separated from God.

But through His Son, Jesus, we have been brought near to Him again. Through Jesus, the separation that once existed between God and man has been done away with. Now, we can come to Him by faith and receive a totally new life that makes our transformation possible.

> *"But the angel reassured them, saying, "Don't be afraid,*
> *for I have come to bring you good news, the most joyous news*
> *the world has ever heard! And it is for everyone everywhere! For today in*
> *Bethlehem a rescuer was born for you. He is the Lord Yahweh, the Messiah."*
> —Luke 2:10–11 (TPT)

I love this scripture because it is a reminder that a relationship with Jesus is for all people. This is such good news—*"the most joyous news the world has ever heard! And it is for everyone everywhere"* (Luke 2:10 TPT). Jesus wants a relationship with *you*—a living, growing, powerful daily walk with you that brings about the transformation you desire! Having a relationship with God is what will help you to live a balanced and productive life.

Consider for a moment how coming to know Jesus Christ has changed and is continuing to change your life. Think about what He has done for you. He loves You so much that He died on a Cross for you so that you could be saved, and so that your sins could be forgiven. He has taken your place and done so much for you. When we receive what He has done and live it out daily, it changes us for our good. It blesses us.

Christ, living within us, helps us to live righteously for Him. His full grace is present within us to bring about His will for our lives. He will help us to be transformed.

Whatever religion you have grown up with or experienced in the past, I pray you can set it aside for a while as you focus solely on your relationship with Jesus Christ and stand on His Word alone. The Bible tells us that coming into a relationship with Jesus is as simple as believing in Him, believing that He is God, that He was raised from the dead, that He has all power and authority. That He can and does perform miracles.

When we know and trust in His Lordship and desire Him to be our God, meaning the manager of our life, we will be saved. By identifying these things, we are saying, "Lord, I trust You. I believe in You. I am going to ask You for permission and seek Your counsel and obey You. I will do what You ask me to do, and I believe and trust that You will give me the power from the Holy Spirit living inside of me to do all that You ask."

Once we enter into this saving, life-changing relationship with the Lord, we begin to discover the wondrous experience of being a friend of Jesus. Can you picture it? Imagine beginning your day with your best friend, the one you love. You look forward to talking with them, having coffee with them, hearing how much they love you, hearing how they believe in you and how they will help you with whatever you need.

This is the relationship Jesus is offering you! His Word is full of encouragement. When you read it, place your name in it. Visualize yourself made righteous by God, empowered by Him. The more you use your mind, your imagination, and your emotions for the glory of God and to experience a relationship with Jesus, the more your connection with Him will grow and the greater the joy you will have in your life.

This is what is meant by coming into a true relationship with the Lord—and it has the power to totally transform us.

Truly Knowing God Transforms Us in Every Area

Knowing Jesus and His Word is so valuable because your beliefs about God and who He has created you to be will affect every area of your life. When you are close to Him, you come to realize how much He loves you and has created you to be unique and to have a purpose. Knowing this is so important to becoming free of wrong beliefs and becoming more like Him.

This process of transforming into His image takes time. You see, the beliefs you have right now are rooted in past experiences and the things you have been taught over the years. Some of those beliefs may be godly, and some may be misconceptions that have held you back from receiving God's best. God wants us to be free of any belief that does not line up with the truth, because these wrong beliefs weigh us down and impact our lives, often on a daily basis.

For example, we all experience rejection at some point in our life, whether it came from a parent, a child, a friend, or coworker. This sense of being rejected is such a heavy burden. Over time, our brains can turn the "I don't love you" message from one person into "no one will ever love you," or "you are not good at this," or "you are not good enough."

God never rejects you! He loves you! Psalm 139:13–16 reminds us that God formed us even while we were still in our mother's womb, and He loves us with an everlasting love.

As we know God and walk in His power, we can overcome thoughts of rejection, of being unloved, of not being good enough. And it also helps us to overcome fear!

In this world, fear is ever lurking and trying to take us down. God helps us to overcome this tactic from the enemy.

> *"God, you're such a safe and powerful place to find refuge!*
> *You're a proven help in time of trouble—*
> *more than enough and always available whenever I need you.*
> *So we will never fear, even if every structure of support were to crumble away.*
> *We will not fear even when the earth quakes and shakes,*
> *moving mountains and casting them into the sea.*
> *For the raging roar of stormy winds and crashing waves*
> *cannot erode our faith in you."*
> **—Psalm 46:1–3 (TPT)**

He tells us not to fear because He is always with us! He is victorious and has no fear. Therefore, as His children who have been given the Holy Spirit to remain with us and help us, we also can experience freedom from fear.

Knowing God heals our past wounds. He gives us great victory and makes us better than we could have ever imagined! Filled with great purpose, we become comforters and healers as we comfort and heal others with the same comfort we have been given by God! (2 Corinthians 1:4)

Yes, we all have experienced pain in this life, some more than others, but nothing is ever wasted with God. What the enemy intended to take you down, God is going to use to lift you up! His purposes are so much bigger than we could have imagined!

Personally, I know from experience that I make a mess of my life on my own. But I don't want my life to be a mess. That's why I value my relationship with Jesus. When He orders my path, I am successful. My life goes well when I allow Him to guide me. Knowing the Lord has changed my life tremendously. Now, I live a faithful life with my husband, and I teach my children the ways of the Lord. I teach others what I have learned, to help heal lives. I love helping people! Jesus and I do this together.

And this kind of spiritual walk isn't only for me, or for a select few. It is for all Christians. You can live a joy-filled, faithful, purposeful life too, as you allow Jesus to work within you and transform you more and more into His image.

Jesus—The Manager of Our Life

Throughout our time on earth, we will always be working on areas of our life. There is always something new to learn, and new ways that we can grow. This is a good thing—especially as we lean upon God's power to fuel our transformation. He wants to be involved in even the smallest details of our daily life, guiding us, encouraging us, and blessing us.

When we first allow God's love to heal us and allow His Holy Spirit and His Word to guide us into His will for our life, the blessings He has for us will flow more naturally to us and through us to those around us. Obeying His will and acting by faith on His instructions won't make us any more saved than we already are, but it brings about success because it positions us to receive good things from Him.

I liken this principle to a child coming to a parent and asking the parent if they can eat their vegetables and do their homework. Imagine how delighted and pleased that parent would be. Of course, the parent is going to say yes, because the child is in alignment with what the parent desires. And the parent will then be able to bless the child more because they will be healthy and have finished their homework—and so now there is more time for fun.

There is a cause and effect to everything we do. There are many people who don't know the Lord, yet they prosper in a certain area because they are practicing godly principles.

Imagine how much better your daily life can be as you know that you are practicing God's Word and using His principles in your life. Remember, God is for you! His Spirit dwells within you. His favor is upon you, and He is ever present in your life. When you know this deep down, it builds a faith in you that is unshakeable. It frees you from fear and enables you to face anything!

Our confident, bold faith in the Lord leads us to take action according to His Word, and this brings about our success. This success is given to us by God, but it comes about as we take action according to His principles.

Think about the sun for a moment. It rises every day of our lives. We don't cause the sun to arise in the morning, but if we get up early, we can view the sunrise and align ourselves to see and experience the beauty of that moment. In the same way, God is the Source of our success. We don't create our success in life. We aren't creating the favor and goodness that He brings about for us. He is the Creator, not us. However, as we arise and line ourselves up with His will, His purposes, and His Word, this will align us with Him, and we will experience the success He already has planned for us.

Following God will impact every area of your life if you allow Him to. Once we choose to invite God to be the manager of our life, we allow His transformation power to work in every area of the Circle. And as we give Him permission to lead us in one area, it will bring positive changes in other areas too.

Are you allowing God into your political views? Parenting? Friendships? Recreation? Occupation? Finances? Marriage? Emotions? Civil rights? Are you becoming more generous?

Where do you spend the bulk of your time, energy, and money? What do you need to release in your life, so that God can give you even better?

Remember, He has said we are to have no other Gods before Him. Choosing God, knowing God and following Him requires sacrifice. Are you willing to get up a little bit earlier to talk with Him? To seek His opinion and direction on matters in your life?

Our flesh is easily moved toward pride and self-sufficiency. I want to assure you that understanding the tools in this course does not remove our need for God and for His Holy Spirit working within us and for us! We are simply aligning ourselves with His will.

Make no mistake—to achieve the godly success you desire, you must cooperate with the Lord and give Him the opportunity to lead you and guide you. You cannot do it alone.

Yes, there are certainly people who experience success without God, but even then, the truth is simply that God has allowed them to receive their heart's desire. What will be sad for them is realizing that there was more than just this life. They may have reaped financial success but failed to honor God and therefore failed in the area of spirituality and relationship with Jesus, thus nullifying any success they achieve.

On the other hand, when you achieve success through your awareness of God and the favor He has given to you, and honor Him in that favor, your heart will be satisfied knowing you fulfilled a purpose to which you were called. God alone will grant you this heavenly success and satisfaction as you seek Him and honor Him in all you do. We give all honor, glory, and praise to Him, and Him alone!

Aligning Our Desires with His Desires

We have desires in our life, and when we are seeking God, we seek what He desires for us more than we seek what we desire. We may want more money, a spouse, or a child, and He may give us those things. He truly does care about the desires of your heart. He is that kind of Father. But sometimes we are so fixated on what we want that we are blinded by our shortsightedness. He desires us to exchange things that may not be in our best interest for the great things He wants in our life, the stuff that will be truly fulfilling!

God desires eternal living water for us! He sees the big picture! He knows what is best for us. Trusting Him and seeking His desire for us before our own will truly fill our cup to overflowing.

Do you desire more of Him and more of the awesome things He has planned for you? Then don't be too shortsighted. Be willing to be flexible to accommodate His plans for your life as you make and set goals. Remember, godly principles work! Align yourself with God and His will, and the blessings will follow.

How do we align ourselves with His will? It begins with allowing Jesus to truly be not only our Savior, but also our Lord. The word *Lord* means the *manager* of our life. Jesus is to be the person who helps dictate what we do. When He is truly our Lord, He's going to direct our path and bring us to places that are good for us.

So, it's important to understand what our relationship with Him is all about. It's about having a new manager in our life, one who loves us more than we can imagine and will direct our paths to healthy decisions which lead to healthy actions. And Jesus wants to be more than your Lord. He wants to be your friend as well, so that you can do life together and so that He can help you fulfill your God-given purpose.

God is so good that He gave us everything we need to be empowered to live a godly life. We see this clearly in the work of the Holy Spirit in our lives. Let's take a look at the power of the Holy Spirit in us as we are transformed from Glory to Glory.

The Holy Spirit

*"But I promise you this—the Holy Spirit will come upon you,
and you will be seized with power."*
—Acts 1:8 (TPT)

Spiritual transformation is only possible by the power of God, which is made manifest in us through the Holy Spirit who dwells within us when we are born again. The Word of God makes it clear that it is the Holy Spirit who equips us for godly success. He teaches us. He speaks to us what God is speaking. He leads us into all truth and gives us wisdom and discernment for what to do in our lives.

He works together with us to guide us into greater freedom in the Lord, so that we are able to fulfill the purpose for which we have been created. Receiving the Holy Spirit is the act of accepting His power to live our lives in Him. When you are operating in His empowerment, you will be amazed by how productive and effective your days become.

The Holy Spirit also draws us into a closer fellowship with the Lord. His presence in our lives daily is vital because the Holy Spirit provides us with the victorious power we need to be transformed more and more into the image of God. Without Him, we will lack the empowerment we need to truly live a pure, holy life in Him. The Holy Spirit makes it possible for us to live the life God intends for us. He works in our lives wherever we need His power to overcome.

When we are operating from a place of power which comes from having the Holy Spirit working in our lives, it transforms us. His empowerment makes it possible for us to think as God thinks. He gives us a new way of seeing our life, recognizing what God is doing in and through us. He provides vision for your life. He brings the Word of God to life for us.

Through the Holy Spirit, you can affirm and believe in your godly identity through faith. In this course, we see this in the Inner Narrations that we write each week. We are aligning ourselves with what God says about us, such as, "I AM powerful. I AM an overcomer in Christ. I AM loved by God. I AM wise and discerning about my purpose and path in life. I AM His child."

These things are already true about who we are in Christ, yet negative circumstances and words from others have crept in to cause us to believe lies instead of truth. Spiritual transformation comes into our lives as we speak and believe what God says about us.

Elijah's Prayer

"At the usual time for offering the evening sacrifice, Elijah the prophet walked up to the altar and prayed, 'O Lord, God of Abraham, Isaac, and Jacob, prove today that you are God in Israel and that I am your servant. Prove that I have done all this at your command. O Lord, answer me! Answer me so these people will know that you, O Lord, are God and that you have brought them back to yourself'."

—1 Kings 18:36–37 (NLT)

This scripture was prayed when Elijah was confronting the false prophets of Baal. His desire was that through the action of God, the people would come to know Him. This is to be our prayer too.

First, we are to pray that God will be glorified in every single thing that we do. As you go about your days, continue to check yourself and ask, "Am I doing this because of my love for others, which will glorify God? Or am I doing this for my fame?" What is the reason you are doing what you do?

Second, we are to pray that others will see Jesus in us. Our actions and our reputation matter because they reflect on God. It influences what others believe about God. Therefore, it is important that you receive your complete healing in the Lord so that your actions will reflect that. For me, I have received the love of God which has transformed my life; therefore, I am careful how I represent God. I don't want to harm His name; therefore, I seek to have a good reputation so that others will see God in me. I am careful with how I live so that others will see Him in me.

Finally, we are to pray that as God is glorified through us and others see Him in us, they will turn to Him. This is our whole purpose. Our ministry and all we do is to lead others to Him.

The Act of Communion

There are several practices the Bible encourages us to engage in—actions that strengthen our spiritual lives daily. We often talk about the power of prayer and worship and reading our Bible, all of which are tremendously life-changing actions. I'd like to focus for a moment on a practice you may not have thought much about before today—the act of communion.

"I have handed down to you what came to me by direct revelation from the Lord himself. The same night in which he was handed over, he took bread and gave thanks. Then he distributed it to the disciples and said, 'Take it and eat your fill. It is my body, which is given for you. Do this to remember me.' He did the same with the cup of wine after supper and said, 'This cup seals the new covenant with my blood. Drink it—and whenever you drink this, do it to remember me.' Whenever you eat this bread and drink this cup, you are retelling the story, proclaiming our Lord's death until he comes."

—**1 Corinthians 11:23–26 (TPT)**

In communion, we are reminded that His body was broken for us, which heals and empowers us to do as He did. We are reminded that He poured His blood out, giving His life for ours. In this act of communion, we are flooded with love for our savior and all He has done for us. We are reminded that Christ lives within us, empowering us with the passion to love and serve others as He did. Our focus is directed to all that is eternal and true now, as you are one with Christ.

Every time you take communion, you are reminded of your life union with the Lord and the love and power that He brings into your life. You can take communion on your own anytime. It doesn't have to be anything fancy. Simply take what you have at hand—water and bread—and say something close to this:

"Lord, thank You that Your body was broken for mine, so that through Your sacrifice, I am made whole. Thank You for loving me. May Your love be fully present in all that I say and do. Help me to use my body to glorify You and to serve others. Thank You, Jesus, for Your blood that was poured out for me. You gave Your life for mine. Help me to sacrifice my life for others. Your Holy Spirit lives inside of me, and I am here representing You. Thank You for Your power living inside of me. Thank You, Lord, for all You have done for me."

I do communion most mornings. I love that time with the Lord. I know God's sacrifice for me on the cross is what perfects me and makes up for every area that I lack. His sacrifice perfects every believer that comes to Him. He does not desire lack for us. As you take communion, allow His Holy Spirit to commune with your spirit and give you everything you need to be in perfect alignment with Him.

Communion is available for you anytime—inviting you to be united with the Lord, and to remember His sacrifice for your wholeness. You can become more like Him, to think like Him, and to offer your life for Him.

As you take communion, listen for His instructions and be willing to obey them. Allow this precious time and connection with Him to empower you to operate in His strength, so that you can walk in the victorious transformation God has for you.

Communion is a reminder and an expression of His power at work in us, cleansing us and setting us free of our sin. As we take communion, we receive by faith what He did for us in His body, which was broken for us, and His blood, which was shed for us. Through His broken body and shed blood, we are forgiven, healed, and delivered into the freedom He has for us.

And as you study this course, I encourage you to take communion daily as well. Engage in the act of remembering what Jesus has done for you, giving thanks, and taking time to contemplate who He is to you, and also connecting daily to the truth about who you are in Him. It's easy to forget this truth as we get busy with our daily lives, but communion offers us an opportunity to be united with Jesus Christ, to remember that He took our place on the cross, the place where we would be without Him.

Is Your Relationship with God Healing and Transforming You?

Our relationship with God is so important, so vital to our healing and transformation, yet it is possible to take this connection for granted. What does it mean to be united with Jesus? Some people may have been raised in a church, without really knowing how to connect with God as I expressed earlier in discussing communion and knowing God daily. In doing so, there is a healing and transformation that happens in a living relationship with God. We receive salvation when asking Christ into our hearts, but our healing and our sanctification or transformation only happens when we allow His Word and Holy Spirit to take up residence in us, taking us into more holy places, thus avoiding the self-destruction of our life.

Let me give you an example story.

Dave, a man claiming to be a Christian, was away from home on a business trip. His marriage was not going so well, and he fell into the temptation of having an affair. A fellow Christian happened to see him and questioned in his heart whether or not Dave really knew the Lord.

His wife later found out and began the proceedings for a divorce, which caused him great distress. Not being able to focus on work, Dave lost his job. Dave would eventually lose everything—his wife, his job, his home, and his self-respect.

Was Jesus really his Lord? Was Dave living in communion with Jesus, thus allowing God to heal him and transform him? During counseling, Dave stated that he "believed in his heart that God raised Jesus from the dead." But did he really "confess with his mouth Jesus as Lord"? Was Dave walking in a living relationship with Jesus, thus receiving the love and healing He offers?

We will never know these answers. Only God will know whether Dave's faith in his heart was real. What we do know, however, is that salvation and our healing or transformation can be two different things. All that we are in Christ takes up residence within us when we receive Him as Lord and Savior—yet we also must grow into these Christlike traits daily, over time, as we walk with the Lord and are transformed, more and more, into His image. As we allow that transformation to take, these traits can be reflected outward, more and more.

We also know that if we truly seek Jesus as Lord, meaning Jesus is the manager of our life, the healer and ultimate life coach who guides us and directs us on the right path of eternal life, we will believe Him and daily seek His love as we commune with Him. We will then have the desires that He has and will continue this daily process of being transformed, becoming more like Christ daily as we allow Him greater residence in our lives. This daily communion with Him strengthens us, equips us, and gives us great power to overcome, and thus others will easily identify us as one who is like Christ in obeying God's Word.

Even in Dave's sin, he never lost God's love. God is there to restore anyone who has messed up, even horribly, if we are willing to turn to Him in faith, truly repent and turn away from our sin, and get back on the path of moving forward in the Lord again (1 John 1:9). In that faithful act of turning to Him, we invite His grace into the situation. When you come to Him for help, God always works all things out for your good, even your messes. As we allow God to be revealed more and more in us each day, the Holy Spirit can work these messes out and make us more like God—bringing about greater transformation and Christlikeness.

Yes, Dave paid a very heavy price for his actions and lost it all. Yet even though he grieved the Holy Spirit, he never lost God's love. It's because of His love for us that transformation is possible!

Let's talk about you now, and your coming into a true and healthy relationship with the Lord Jesus Christ. You have heard about what Jesus has done for you, how much He loves you and that He died for you so you could have eternal life. Now comes the time that you believe in your heart and confess with your mouth that Jesus is Lord—meaning you share the Good News about Jesus Christ and what He has done for the world—so that you can be saved. The gift of His salvation is yours through faith in Him, and through His grace toward you.

If this is true for you—if you believe in Him and have confessed Him as Lord and Savior of your life—then you are saved. You will be with Jesus for all eternity! He loves you and cares for you. If you really love Jesus, you will not grieve Him by how you represent Him to the world. You are now married to Him, and your life needs to change accordingly because of your love for Him. Jesus wants all of you! He is a jealous God. The good news is, giving ourselves wholly to Him is so worth it. He will never let us down.

The Transforming Work of Sanctification

Some of the questions arising around spirituality center around the difference between *salvation*—the act of receiving by faith the gift of new life that Jesus Christ won for us on the cross—and *sanctification*—the ongoing practice of becoming more holy and pure in Him as we become more like Him every day.

It's important to recognize that our salvation comes through faith in the Lord, and it is His gift of grace to us. We don't save ourselves; He has already done the work. Our part is to agree, by faith, and receive what He has already done for us, by faith. We will never be more saved that we are the day we open our hearts to receive Him as Lord and Savior.

Still, we have much growing to do. Once we come to know the Lord, we can begin to learn more about His ways of doing things, of being in the world, of interacting with others.

God's truth may be quite different from the way you have been taught to do things in the past, from your parents, from teachers, and from the world in general. Your thought patterns, beliefs and habits may not have aligned with His ways.

As you come into a relationship with Jesus, it requires time and dedication to discover what He says about you are, to be honest with yourself about what must change and areas where you must grow to be like Him. This is the work of sanctification in our lives.

As we trust the Lord with these areas of life, the Holy Spirit will help us in our ongoing transformation into His likeness. The more we give ourselves to studying the Bible, opening our heart to Him, and engaging in activities like this Bible study—and the more we learn about His power within us—the more we can be transformed into His image.

The Great Commission—God's Ultimate Purpose for Us

Our transformation into God's image is to be a blessing to us, of course. But it also has a deeper purpose that God has called us to. As we are transformed to be like Him, we are empowered to bring His life-changing message to the world, to our families, to our friends and coworkers, and everyone we meet. Sharing the Gospel is an essential part of our spiritual life.

The Great Commission is the great co-mission—meaning it is a partnership with both man and God! We are called to go into all the world and preach the Gospel. This call is for everyone, every Christian, and it is to reach out to all people with what is true. You cannot go to heaven or access God without belief.

Believing in Christ is the most important transformation we'll make, and we are privileged to be called to share this belief with others, so they also can come to Christ and be transformed!

Faith is like a light switch that operates by motion. It is activated when we move. You will get what you believe for! The miracles of God happen for those who believe. And your faith unlocks the power.

Many Christians play it safe, and they do not step out in faith. God honors our faith when we step out to share the Gospel with others. You will grow spiritually when first you learn from the Lord and then step out and share what you have learned. Your spiritual maturity is not based on how many scriptures you know, but on how you share what you learn.

If we want to see success in the area of our spirituality, we have to step out in faith! God is present with goers and doers! God wants to speak to you and through you!

I think of faith as being spelled RISK. If I do nothing, I risk nothing, but I also know what to expect—which is nothing. But if I have faith and take a risk, God can show up! In fact, He has promised to show up as we share the Gospel. Our part is to step out in faith, open our mouths and preach, pray for the sick, and bless others.

As we do, God's Word promises that signs and wonders will follow those who believe. We'll help others to improve their lives! We will help others heal as we pray for them. We will help others come to know of the love of the Lord and how He healed our lives and how He can heal theirs! These are the signs, wonders and miracles that Jesus speaks of, and they remind us of the goodness of God. This is the Good News Gospel!

Bringing Greater Success to Your Spiritual Life

What we believe in our heart is what will come out of our mouth. Our belief is what we will confess to the world. Ask yourself what you are passionate about. What has transformed in your life? As you apply the 5 Keys to Success (described in Week One) in all areas of your life, you can grow, improve, and become passionate about that truth and share it with others!

What is the truth about you in your spiritual life? Take a look at what you believe and your daily habits. Are you getting into God's Word regularly? Are you praying regularly? Are you believing that God is going to answer you today and give you a word of direction today?

Only you can answer that. Yes, God knows you better than you know yourself. But there isn't a therapist, or a coach, or a spouse who knows you better than you know yourself. You know what your purposes and intents are, how much time you are spending with Him, and whether your focus is on the Lord or elsewhere. And as we ask Him to search us and reveal what is in our heart, He will show us what is true about our spiritual life.

What is your goal with the Lord? Is your goal to be connected with Him? To honor and please Him? To bring others to Him? There's always a big picture goal of living forever with Him as a child of God in His kingdom. And then there are smaller goals too, personal goals we may have at any given time. We can assess ourselves to see what we desire to accomplish.

As you consider these smaller goals, remember to consider the purpose behind them, because your purpose motivates you toward accomplishing those goals. For example, perhaps you have decided that you would like to spend more time in prayer, and to do so, you must get up 15–20 minutes earlier than normal. Your purpose is what will drive you to get up when you want to remain in bed.

So, be clear on your purpose. Perhaps it is that spending time in prayer encourages you and helps you to be more joyful and peaceful. Joy and peace are a wonderful reason to get up early, isn't it? You can see how knowing that purpose can make it easier for you to be committed to doing what it takes to achieve your goals.

Next, consider the plan that will work for you, and the action steps to help you get there. Rising early is one way to achieve this goal, but it's not the only way. For some people, it may be better to take time at lunch for prayer, or before bedtime. Choose the plan that will work best for you right now in your current season of life.

To help you accomplish the plan, you must be clear on your action steps. Perhaps you may decide to take the additional action of setting your alarm. You may even decide to go to bed earlier, so that it is easier to get up earlier, or turn off the TV at a set time so you can spend time in prayer before you go to sleep. These simple action steps are the elements of your plan for achieving your goal—all so that you can enjoy the results of your purpose, which is to be more joyful in the Lord.

Accountability is also useful in helping us achieve our goals. Some people have a spouse who is a strong Christian who can act as an accountability partner. Others may need to look for a godly friend or a life coach to play that role. It's important to select someone who has a close walk with the Lord. Whoever you choose, explain to them what you are doing and how they can help support you in accomplishing your goals. Be sure your accountability partner is someone who will check in with you regularly, encourage you and equip you to grow even more by asking you questions.

For example, a great accountability partner might ask you if you are following through with your plans of waking up early or taking time before bed to pray. They may ask you to share any insights you are having, any challenges, and any successes. These conversations equip you to evaluate how you are doing and allow you to adjust as needed to move toward more success.

As you take these steps to daily evaluate and make any necessary adjustments in your spiritual life, you will begin to see the rewards of your efforts and find greater freedom and success in your walk with the Lord. And you'll see His blessings come about in your life as a result.

There is one final thought I'd like to leave you with. As we are getting to know the Lord and developing our spiritual connection with Him, thus improving our spiritual life, we have to set aside everything we think we know about earthly relationships. Often, we are looking to experience God with our five senses through our experiences in this world. We must learn to use our spiritual senses, to see with eyes of understanding, to hear with spiritual ears God's voice from His Word, to gain an internal spiritual depth that brings an understanding the world does not know.

True worshippers worship God in spirit. They also commune in spirit. They see, hear, touch, taste and smell with their spiritual senses. And you can grow stronger in this ability and become more like Him as you are transformed more and more into His image.

Week Two : Spirituality

Day 1

Spirituality
Coming into a Relationship with Jesus

"And what is God's 'living message'? It is the revelation of faith for salvation, which is the message that we preach. For if you publicly declare with your mouth that Jesus is Lord and believe in your heart that God raised him from the dead, you will experience salvation. The heart that believes in him receives the gift of the righteousness of God—and then the mouth confesses, resulting in salvation."
—**Romans 10:9–10 (TPT)**

Is the above scripture really all it takes to come into a transformative relationship with Jesus?

I'd like to answer that with an example:

If two people decide to get married and each confesses the words "I do," you will be married. But the act of getting married isn't the same as maintaining a healthy marriage that honors both spouses. If you choose to engage in behavior that harms your spouse, they will still be grieved.

In the same way, you can grieve the Lord by the way you relate to Him and how you represent your marriage to Him. To have a healthy relationship with Him, we make choices every day that are good and godly. If we don't, we will grieve Him. If there are areas where you have grieved Him, ask for forgiveness! Ask Him to forgive you, repent and make the necessary changes. Continue to ask God to search your heart and show you where you need to make changes.

Today, take time to consider what it means to you to be in a relationship with Jesus. Consider where you currently are on the scale of being close to Him, living in ways that are pleasing to Him. This act of examining ourselves equips us to be intentional and purposeful in our daily spiritual walk with God. It makes space for us to experience gratitude for what He has already done in our lives, and to acknowledge what can be brought to Him prayerfully for our growth and continued transformation into His image.

Gain Insight

Answer the questions, be honest with yourself and be transformed!

1. How does coming to know Jesus Christ and what He has done for you change the way you feel about Him? About yourself?

   _____

   _____

   _____

2. What is the reason you desire a relationship with Jesus?

3. How will having this relationship change your life? How does it perfect you?

4. What are some of the things you plan to do with Jesus?

5. What if people don't like your relationship with Jesus?

Pray

Lord, I desire to be closer to You. Help me to get to know You better. Help me to get to know myself better. You know me better than anyone. I desire to be in Your will, Lord Jesus, to walk in the fullness that You have for me. I know that You came to bring me life! Help me to be aware of anything that would seek to take that away.

Day 2

Spirituality
Baptism

*"Peter replied, 'Repent and return to God,
and each one of you must be baptized in the name of Jesus,
the Anointed One, to have your sins removed.
Then you may take hold of the gift of the Holy Spirit'."*
—**Acts 2:38 (TPT)**

As a believer in Jesus Christ, I love the Lord. If you also love the Lord, you will have a desire to display that love. This is the purpose of baptism. It is an outward expression of the inward love that we feel toward Jesus.

The act of baptism is such a powerful expression of your faith in Him. You wouldn't be married to someone without having a marriage ceremony, would you?

It is the same with our relationship to Jesus. Baptism is an outward expression of our inward relationship and connection with Him, something that acts to show the world, and ourselves, that we have made a genuine and lasting commitment to God. It announces to the world what God has done within us.

Being baptized is so honoring to the Lord. It shows everyone that we are proud and grateful to be in a relationship with Him. If you haven't had an opportunity to be baptized in the Lord yet, I highly encourage you to do so.

Gain Insight

Answer the questions, be honest with yourself and be transformed!

1. What is the purpose of baptism?

2. What does your baptism mean to you?

3. Have you received the gift of the Holy Spirit?

4. Do you regularly take communion, taking time to reflect on and remember your baptism in the Lord and the presence of the Holy Spirit in your life?

5. Would you like to see others get baptized because of your good influence?

Pray

Lord, give me courage to be baptized and show the world that I belong to You. Help me to walk in the power of the Holy Spirit and to honor You in all that I do. Help me to be a good influence on others and bring them into Your fold through baptism.

Day 3

Spirituality
Learning His Ways

"Those who say they live in God should live their lives as Jesus did."
—1 John 2:6 (NLT)

We transform our thinking through our daily interactions with God's Word. In it, we find all the key spiritual principles we need, which guide us successfully through life.

Consider this: If we are to be like Jesus, we must first know what He is like. The Bible is filled with scriptures that tell us who God is, what Jesus did and does for us, and who we are in Him. This may be familiar to you, or it may be very new, depending on how long you have known the Lord. (In the Appendix, you will find a list of scriptures that tell us who we are in Him.)

Of course, we all are continuing to be transformed in Him, and we all learn and grow so that we can become more like Him. The Word of God will continue to reveal greater depths of truth about the Lord to us as we engage daily with it through prayer, study, meditation and times of praise and worship.

"All Scripture is breathed out by God and profitable for teaching, for reproof, for correction, and for training in righteousness" (2 Timothy 3:16 ESV). God's Word has been given to us for a reason. *"It will empower you by its instruction and correction, giving you the strength to take the right direction and lead you deeper into the path of godliness"* (2 Timothy 3:16 TPT). It provides us with the knowledge and understanding we need to make godly decisions. And the more we line ourselves up with what He tells us to do, the more success we will experience.

God has given us what we need in His Word to live for Him. Our part is to use His Word daily, to initiate His power to accomplish the dreams, goals, and purposes He has placed within us.

This becomes especially valuable as we face situations that we must overcome, and areas of our life where we need His power to be transformed. Yes, hope is a good thing, and we should have hope for good things to come.

But hope is not enough on its own to produce success. We're in a battle, and we must use the sword of the Spirit, the Word of God, by faith to take hold of the victory God has for us. Speaking His Word out of our mouths and declaring it in faith over our lives is one of the most powerful spiritual weapons for transformation that He has given us.

Gain Insight

Answer the questions, be honest with yourself and be transformed!

1. How can you learn more of Jesus' Ways?

2. What are some of the characteristics of Jesus Christ?

3. What are some of the things you would like to change to become more like Christ?

4. Is your relationship better with Jesus when you are more like Him?

5. Does it grieve Him when you are not?

Pray

Lord, help me to spend time with You, learning Your ways. Give me more of Your character as I come into Your presence. Help me to love as You love, to forgive as You forgive and to live as You live.

Day 4

Spirituality
Godly Mind

"Keep your thoughts continually fixed on all that is authentic and real, honorable and admirable, beautiful and respectful, pure and holy, merciful and kind. And fasten your thoughts on every glorious work of God, praising him always."
—Philippians 4:8 (TPT)

There is nothing better in life than having a godly mind. What does it mean to have a godly mind? For starters, it is to think as Philippians 4:8 tells us.

So many times, our thoughts are anywhere else but on what this verse of scripture describes. This world we live in can make it hard to do so. The secular world focuses on what is negative, what is ugly, what is terrifying. Just consider the nightly news for an example. So much of the news is focused on what is going wrong with our world.

But such thoughts do not empower us. They do not help us to live joyfully, confidently, and purposefully. We must guard our minds and counter negative lies and doubts with what is true and good, so that we can stay focused on what God has created us to be and do.

We are to think on what is noble and what is lovely, such as charity and justice and generosity. As we think in our hearts, so we will be in our daily activities (Proverbs 23:7). If we want to walk in confidence, in victory, in joy and peace, then we must begin by thinking thoughts that encourage us to be bold, strong, and filled with hope and faith in the Lord.

One way to do this is to think on the beautiful things God has created for us to enjoy. There are so many wonderful things He has made. Picture in your mind the gorgeous Alps, the warm beaches of the Bahamas, the stunning colors of all the flowers He has created. Look at all the wonderful cultures and people God has made! It is so much fun seeing the creative things that God has made. And it is encouraging and uplifting.

Remember, He made you too! And you are more beautiful than anything else He has made.

Think also about the creativity God has placed within you. What are the creative things you like to do? Do you enjoy painting, crafting, making clothes, or planting a garden? These are all creative things God can give us to do, and these are lovely, wonderful things to think on.

Week Two : Spirituality

Gain Insight

Answer the questions, be honest with yourself and be transformed!

1. What are some of the good things in this world?

2. What are some of the things in nature you enjoy?

3. What cultures or places in the world cause you to think about how creative God is?

4. What creative things do you enjoy?

5. What are some of the noble things others have done?

Pray

Lord, everything that is good and true is from You. Help me to stay focused on all the good things in this world, and the good promises You have for me. Help me to keep godly vision for my life, to see myself the way You see me, to surround myself with people like You. May every thought I think be thoughts You would desire for me to have. I love You, Lord. Thank You for all the lovely things You have shown me.

Day 5

Spirituality
Representing Jesus

*"But you are God's chosen treasure —priests who are kings,
a spiritual 'nation' set apart as God's devoted ones.
He called you out of darkness to experience his marvelous light,
and now he claims you as his very own. He did this so that you would
broadcast his glorious wonders throughout the world."*
—**1 Peter 2:9 (TPT)**

When we have the Lord as the new manager in our life, one who loves us and gives us great power, we become passionate about the excellent things He has done for us, and we cannot help but share this good news with others!

This beautiful empowerment is a representation to the world of what they, too, can have by coming to know Jesus. We then become known as someone who has much to offer this hungry world. God's grace changes us, and we desire more so we can represent Him well to others. To represent someone is to re-present that individual to the world. The more you reflect God and His grace, the more you will effectively re-present Christ to others.

First John 4:17 (TPT) tells us, *"…all that Jesus now is, so are we in this world."* We are to become like Jesus in this world, in our daily lives. Everywhere we go, we are to be His hands and His feet and His voice. This is how we influence others for their good.

Our transformation is so valuable because it is purposeful! As we are transformed from Glory to Glory, we become more and more like Jesus. We more easily operate out of the power that the Holy Spirit provides us.

As Christians, we are members of a royal priesthood. Do you realize that as a child of the King, you are a member of His royal family and also a member of His priesthood? In this role as kings and priests of our God, we are called to show forth to the world the nature and will of the Lord, doing good and walking in His power in our daily lives. We are called to accomplish great things, leading and sharing Him with others.

We often see Jesus in others, yet we may not see Him in ourselves. And we suffer when we don't have a clear vision of Jesus within us. It can make us harsher and more judgmental of ourselves, which can stand in the way of our transformation.

So, I encourage you to begin to see yourself as Jesus sees you. Visualize for a moment what it means to be a child of the King of Kings. Create a picture in your mind of what that would be like. How does it feel to be so incredibly loved? What are you wearing? How are you speaking? What would you be saying and doing?

This is your true self. It is who you are and who you are meant to be. As you begin to walk more closely with Him, giving attention to your spiritual life each day, you will grow in your vision for who you are in Him.

Gain Insight

Answer the questions, be honest with yourself and be transformed!

1. Since Jesus is our great High Priest, how do you feel about your royal priesthood?

2. Do you realize you have been made worthy of the priesthood you have been given?

3. In what ways does this cause you to be transformed and represent Jesus well?

4. What are some of the excellent things God has done in your life?

5. What are some ways that you can draw closer to Jesus and keep yourself holy and pure?

___

___

___

Pray

Lord, You have brought me out of darkness into Your marvelous light! Thank You for your grace and love. Thank You for gifting me with a royal priesthood to be a blessing to others. Help me continue to walk in Your power with purity and purpose, helping and blessing others and teaching them Your ways.

Day 6

Spirituality
Helping Others

"'For when you saw me hungry, you fed me. When you found me thirsty, you gave me drink. When I had no place to stay, you invited me in, and when I was poorly clothed, you covered me. When I was sick, you tenderly cared for me, and when I was in prison you visited me.' Then the godly will answer him, 'Lord, when did we see you hungry or thirsty and give you food and something to drink? When did we see you with no place to stay and invite you in? When did we see you poorly clothed and cover you? When did we see you sick and tenderly care for you, or in prison and visit you?' And the King will answer them, 'Don't you know? When you cared for one of the least of these, my little ones, my true brothers and sisters, you demonstrated love for me.'"
—Matthew 25:35–40 (TPT)

As you come into a deeper relationship with Jesus, you will gain a desire to share the good news with others. This is your purpose as a believer! Spreading the good news and helping others in their life is the greatest joy and purpose that we can have. You will find your passion for life and others increasing the more and more you are flooded with the love of God and His Holy Spirit working within you. You will find yourself reaching out to make a difference in the lives of those you encounter.

There are so many ways you can help others! You can smile, bless them, and give them a word of encouragement. You can pray for them, carry their bags to their car, and listen to them when they need someone to talk to. You can make them a meal or offer to help them pick out a new outfit at the store. There is always a way to help someone; even the smallest things you do to bless others can make a tremendous impact on them.

Yes, you! You can make a difference!

Because you have been redeemed, you can do what no one else can! You will reach people that others cannot. You will be filled with purpose to partner with Jesus and bring others to Him to be set free.

Gain Insight

Answer the questions, be honest with yourself and be transformed!

1. What are some of the ways you have helped others?

Week Two: Spirituality

2. What are some ways you would like to serve others?

3. How do you feel when you are helping?

4. Does it bring you closer to Jesus when you are serving the least?

5. How does it change those you have helped?

Pray

Lord, break my heart for what breaks Yours. Help me to be kind, considerate and helpful. Help me to be the example that You called me to be so that I do not cause another to stumble. Open my mind as I continue to read Your Word, the Bible. Give me clarity and direction and more inspiration to bless others.

Day 7

Spirituality
Sabbath Rest

"So we conclude that there is still a full and complete Sabbath-rest waiting for believers to experience. As we enter into God's faith-rest life we cease from our own works, just as God celebrates his finished works and rests in them. So then we must be eager to experience this faith-rest life, so that no one falls short by following the same pattern of doubt and unbelief."
—**Hebrews 4:9–10 (TPT)**

Our discussion of spirituality isn't complete until we talk about a final area in which many Christians struggle—and that is the area of resting.

Many of us find it hard to simply rest. Many are workaholics. Constantly trying to work your way up in society and being successful in the world's eyes is exhausting, and it can be a type of idol. This is not God's best for you.

God desires rest for you. Knowing God and trusting Him helps us to distinguish the pace and pursuits of our lives, what to do—and what not to do. We are not like the unbelievers who do not understand true contentment and peace in the Lord. We have the great privilege and blessing of knowing that He will provide for us, that He will answer our prayers.

Every day of the week, we are to have a time to rest. God has commanded us to enjoy a sabbath rest, which restores us and refreshes us and allows us to evaluate ourselves and make new plans. While many people think of rest as a physical act, it is very much a spiritual act as well.

During times that we rest in the Lord and spend time with Him, He can work in us to give us a new mind and a new heart for the purposes He has called us to. It is in these times of rest that He restores our soul and renews our strength.

*"I stand silently to listen for the one I love,
waiting as long as it takes for the Lord to rescue me.
For God alone has become my Savior.
He alone is my safe place; his wraparound presence always protects me.
For he is my champion defender; there's no risk of failure with God"*
—**Psalm 62:1–2 (TPT)**

When we rest on the Sabbath, we are trusting and surrendering to God, knowing He will work everything out for our good! We rest not only on the Sabbath, but in every situation, knowing He is with us, and He has overcome it all.

Gain Insight

Answer the questions, be honest with yourself and be transformed!

1. What are some of the ways you can rest your body?

2. What can you do today to rest your mind?

3. In what ways will you allow God to refresh your spirit?

4. What has God done for you to give you perfect rest?

5. Is it possible to do an activity and still feel restored?

Pray

Lord Jesus, help me to rest in You. May all that I do today refresh my body, mind, and spirit. Even when there are times I must do an activity or chore, help me to do it unto You so that I may feel refreshed and have the peace that comes only from You. Guide my ways and direct my paths to keep my whole-self rested in You. Thank You for Your finished work that brings me peace.

Reflection for the Week on Spirituality

Answer the questions, be honest with yourself and be transformed!

1. Are you moving closer to your spiritual goals?

2. Is there anything getting in the way?

3. Do you need to set any new plans?

4. Have you found an accountability partner?

5. In what ways can you help someone in their spiritual life?

Write Your Inner Narration

As you learn more about God and His Word, and as you answer the questions this week, there will be things you discover that you can add to your narration so you can become more and more like Christ.

Using what you have learned from this chapter, the scriptures you have memorized this week, and what you discovered while answering this week's questions, build on your original narration from week 1 and write an additional short godly narration using only positive words. If you find it helpful, review your answers to the daily questions from this week, take note of any positive words, and include them in your new godly narration for this week.

Example: I AM beautiful. I AM loved by God, just as I AM.
I AM forgiven. I AM pleasing to God. I AM strong. I AM courageous.

I AM filled with godly purpose. I AM equipped and able to achieve my godly goals.
I AM a son or a daughter of the King. I AM covered in His grace.
Nothing anyone says or does can harm me because I AM protected … etc.

Week Three

Relationships

If there is one thing that human beings tend to have in common, it is that we long to find the right companions and form relationships that are meaningful to us. It is rare to find people who truly desire to be completely alone all the time, perhaps because God has created us to have companionship—family, friends, spouses, coworkers, and others who are within our sphere of influence. From the beginning of our creation, humans have been created to enjoy good, godly connections with others that build us up, encourage us, and give us opportunities to be a blessing as we are blessed.

Often, I coach and work with those who are navigating challenging situations with those they are connected to. It's not unusual for people to find themselves at odds with others, experiencing a lack of harmony that is stressful and painful. These times may be momentary, or they may last for days, months, even years as we may find ourselves repeating cycles of behaviors that keep us stuck.

God's desire for us, though, is much different. He has created us for strong, positive connections that bless us and help us to fulfill our purpose. I love how the image of the Cross reflects His plan in this area of life. The Cross is first vertical, indicating that God pours into our lives first. And then it is horizontal, reaching out to the world with what we have to offer, because we have been filled to overflowing.

As we learn to let go of limiting beliefs and align ourselves with the truth about who He has created us to be, our transformation into His image will open pathways to healthier relationships.

Being Our True Self in Our Relationships

If there is one word that sums up how we can successfully relate to the people in our life, it's *authenticity*. This isn't just being ourselves; it is being the true, born-again self that God intends us to be when we are *in Christ*. This means being all the things that God has described us to be in Galatians 5:22–23 as He talks about the fruit of the Spirit—being genuine, honest, loving and kind, peaceful, patient, virtuous, full of godly joy and faith. Being authentically ourselves *in Christ* means living out of our Christlike attributes.

As we live like Christ intends, we begin to find it easier to make good decisions about how we interact in our relationships. This Christ-like authenticity stems from the godly, biblical belief systems we hold about ourselves and other people. Transforming our thinking is so valuable to creating the godly beliefs and Christlikeness that will allow us to show forth His light, be our best selves, and be blessed in our relationships.

This may seem hard to imagine at first, because we live in a world where people are often trying too hard to be everything else but themselves. But God wants you to heal, grow, and be transformed into your full potential *in Christ*. As we are aligned with what is true about ourselves as God sees us, it becomes easier to be open and honest with others, kind, and patient, willing to forgive and ask for forgiveness, good at setting healthy boundaries—all the things that make our relationships better!

This also flows into the other areas of our lives, such as our finances, our jobs, and so on; the more we improve one area, the more other areas are blessed as well. Our beliefs about ourselves and others therefore impact all our relationships, which then impact other areas of life. So, I'll repeat this: It's important to be rooted in knowing who we are in Christ.

When we have belief systems that are based on past trauma, pain, or dysfunction rather than our Christlike selves, this can cause us to develop a false persona of who we are and how we relate to others. In other words, as we interact with others, we find that we're not really being who God created us to be—loving, wise, courageous, and so much more.

Instead, we often try to be who we think others want us to be. To survive the dysfunctional family we belonged to, or to get through past traumatic experiences, we may have learned to behave in ways that are overly accommodating, too hostile, or otherwise are simply not allowing us to be our best and most authentic self. We take on roles that are not a fit for who God created us to be. To try to please others, we find ourselves making choices that are not good for us.

These false personas—the good girl, the black sheep, the problem child, and so on—are a defense mechanism that arises as a result of what we have experienced. They are meant to protect us, yet they often hinder our success. In the long run, focusing our efforts on trying to be who others want us to be won't help us build good relationships. It tends to drive us away from who God has originally created us to be, making it difficult to bring our best selves into situations.

Trying to be someone you are not can be exhausting. When that is coupled with hiding your truth to avoid shame, it becomes bondage. Dishonesty is more than telling lies. It is reflective of a broken, dysfunctional human being who needs healing. It reveals a life that operates on people-pleasing, fear of rejection, and fear of the unknown.

The good news is that whatever has brought you to a point of dishonesty in your life can be healed. Do not let the enemy keep you stuck. Jesus wants to heal you.

When we are honest about ourselves and our relationships, this means we are taking a look at how we are communicating, how much service we are offering, and how we are relating to those around us. For change to occur, it's essential to know the *truth* about where we are right now—which is the first of the 5 keys to success in our YKI method of coaching.

Being honest and knowing the truth about your relationships can significantly improve your relationships. Now, I cannot promise you that everyone you are honest with will stay. It is inevitable that some may need time to heal if they feel betrayed. And others may not be safe to completely reveal all things to. You do not have to tell all things to all people. It is wise to turn to God for guidance about what to reveal to others and when. The Holy Spirit will guide you in this as you turn to Him and seek His help.

Know that the freedom you will feel from living true to God and yourself will be worth the changes that occur, as good can only come from living authentically and obediently to God. You will be free from the bondage you were in from the belief systems that held you captive.

As you experience greater freedom in the Lord, you will also gain a greater ability to be flexible as you fulfill all the roles you have in life. You'll be able to draw upon the power and authority of Christ within you to be the best person you can be in each of your many different roles and relationships.

Yes, I know there are many characters you must play to fulfill all your needed positions for so many in your life. I get it! You must humble yourself and become patient with the small child in your life that you are attending to. You must be stern for the teenager in need of boundaries. You must calmly explain the task at hand for those who need to understand. God desires to help us to operate in His grace, strength, and power in all these situations and more.

Fortunately, with Jesus as our role model, the one who is both the lion and the lamb, we can learn from Him how to successfully take on different roles and still be authentically ourselves in Christ. As we renew our minds to align with His truths, we can be transformed—and so can our relationships, bringing us priceless peace and joy.

God's Way to Create Balance in Our Relationships

"'Teacher, which commandment in the law is the greatest?'
Jesus answered him,
'Love the Lord your God with every passion of your heart,
with all the energy of your being, and with every thought that is within you.'
This is the great and supreme commandment.
And the second is like it in importance:
'You must love your friend in the same way you love yourself.'"
—Matthew 22:36–39 (TPT)

You've probably heard this scripture before, but you may be wondering how to apply it in your life in a way that is healthy. For example, you may have had parents or guardians who taught you that you must look out for your own interests, and not worry about the needs of others. Or, you may have been in an unhealthy relationship with someone who repeatedly told you that it was selfish to take care of yourself. Perhaps they made you feel ashamed if you were not constantly giving them all your time and energy.

Relationships that are not balanced can drain us, frustrate us, and impede our ability to enjoy the success we long to experience. When our relationships are not placed in proper order, they may cause us to be out of balance, thus affecting other areas of our lives.

Note, too, that unhealthy relationships that cannot be restored may need to be moved to a great distance so that we can be healthy in body, mind, and spirit.

Thankfully, God in His wisdom has provided us with a biblical order of how we can structure our relationships so that we can make good decisions, build ourselves up in the Lord, gain the balance we need, and be equipped to bless others. This order is as follows:

1. God comes first in our relationships, as all the issues of life flow out of our heart. When our heart is connected to Him, we remain healthy, which helps us in every area.

2. Caring for ourselves comes next, so that we can be strong, balanced, and equipped to do what we are called to do.

3. Finally, we care for others through the overflow that is created in our lives as God fills us and places the correct passions on our heart.

Depending upon your family of origin, your past experiences with other people, and what you have been taught to believe, this order of relationships may seem strange or uncomfortable. You may even be thinking it seems selfish to put yourself on the list at all. But it is so valuable to care for yourself, so you can be refreshed and able to generously care for others.

Keep in mind that what God desires for us is good because He is good. As you learn the rhythms of His grace in our lives, you will find the wisdom in His design of placing Him first, ourselves next, and then others. Let's look more closely at how this divine order of relationships allows us to enjoy the blessings of God and be a blessing to others as He intends.

God First: The Rock on Which We Stand

The entire center of our creation and our purpose begins with our Creator—God Himself. Romans 8:28 (NLT) says, *"And we know that God causes everything to work together for the good of those who love God and are called according to his purpose for them."* The Passion Translation says it like this: *"So we are convinced that every detail of our lives is continually woven together for good, for we are his lovers who have been called to fulfill his designed purpose."* Naturally, this good plan He created for us includes our relationships.

God has a purpose for us in our relationships! But it is difficult to recognize and fulfill His purpose if we don't spend time building up our connection with Him. As we grow closer to Him, we can begin to draw more frequently on His wisdom. We can renew our minds to the truth in His Word and lean on the help of the Holy Spirit to make good decisions that benefit the people in our lives. What a great blessing that is!

As you draw near to the Lord and allow Him to speak into your life, He will transform you more and more into who He has created you to be. And this allows your God-given purpose to come to the forefront of your life, so you can live it out successfully. You and those you are close to will benefit when you are being your true, best, godly self.

It is also valuable and wise to put God first in every area of life, as this positions us to receive His help to resolve issues that arise. After all, every area of life has occasional challenges, including our families, our friendships, and other relationships. As we put the Lord first and seek Him, He meets us where we are at and becomes all that we need. Through Him, we can gain what is required to win the needed battles and bring peace into all our relationships.

Self-Care: Building Ourselves Up So We Have Something to Give

True self-care is spending time with God, as He is the one who refreshes our body, mind, and spirit. He will give you the wisdom on how to love and care for yourself. Taking good, godly care of yourself is **not** a selfish act. In fact, it is an essential key to helping you to be all God has called you to be. You are so important to the Lord! He values you so greatly. It is healthy and spiritual to appreciate your value, just as He does.

When we feel healthy and well, we are better able to get along with other people. We see benefits in our relationships when we also care for our personal needs in a godly way—taking care of our body so we can act from a place of health, taking care of our mind so we can act from a place of emotional health, and taking care of our spirit through spending time with God and learning from Him. We will reflect this health and well-being in the way we treat others. We will become healthier and more balanced in every area. This means we have more to offer to those we are in relationship with.

This is such good news! Self-care is not only for our own benefit, but also for the benefit of others.

Remember, what is happening in one area of our life affects the others. When we do not take good care of our financial wellness, for example, it becomes hard to bless someone by buying them lunch or a coffee. When we are not caring for our physical wellness, we can lack the energy or health we need to visit with someone in their time of need. When we are not spending time with the Lord in prayer, it can become more difficult to sense His prompting when He would have us help someone. We might find ourselves feeling less patient with our spouse and our children.

On the other hand, when we care for ourselves well, we gain the resources and strength and confidence to be there for people when they need us. We'll have so much wisdom and energy to draw upon as we interact with our spouse, child, parents, friends, coworkers, employers, and others. Good self-care is a great way of ensuring we are ready to create strong relationships with those in our sphere of influence.

How do you practice good self-care? Remember our YKI principle—You Know It! Ask yourself what you need right now. Do you need rest? A healthy meal? Fresh water? A calming walk outdoors? A brief break to pray, to read an encouraging scripture, or worship the Lord? All these activities are wonderful ways to care for yourself.

Loving Others Well

In the English language, there's only one word for "love"—and this tends to result in confusion about how God intends us to be in our relationships with others. We can feel as though we are to love everyone in the very same way, with exactly the same level of commitment. And when we don't, it can bring shame and guilt because we may feel we're not living up to what God has commanded us to do.

When God said, *"Love your neighbor as yourself,"* what did He mean? I believe the way He gave this instruction to us is a blessing, because He could have easily said, "Love the world as you love yourself." But He didn't phrase it that way because loving the entire world is too much for one human being to do. God sacrificed Himself on the Cross for the world, so that everyone who believed would have eternal life. He is big enough to love the world.

But humans have limits. We cannot be available to everyone equally. Of course, we are to be filled with the love of God and let that love influence how we interact with others. But we are not interacting with the entire world daily. Instead, we're in relationship with certain people regularly. For the purposes here, we'll consider our neighbors to be our sphere of influence—our family, our friends, our coworkers, our fellow church members, our schoolmates, and anyone else we come into contact with.

When we love others well, we reap a great reward in each area of our lives. Our career will go more smoothly. We'll have greater peace and freedom in our emotional life. It'll be easier to find energy to put toward our physical wellness. We'll experience the joy intended for us because we are managing our relationships as God intended.

Managing Our Sphere of Influence: Inner and Outer Circles

We all have important connections with those around us—spouses, children, friends, coworkers, business partners, teammates—and they all require our presence. Many people can try too hard to do it all—being friends with everyone, doing ministry, being available to anyone in need, volunteering, taking calls from extended family members at any time of the day or night, working, and so on. This can drain us of so much time and energy, which is not good for our relationships.

Yet there is only so much time in the day, and we have only so much energy and so much capacity for relationships. That means we cannot do it all. We must choose who will receive more of our time, and who will receive less. Therefore, it's important to know how to manage our time well and how to govern our relationships.

The proper order for our relationships, according to the Scriptures, is clear. God comes first. Then, our spouse, followed by our children, and very close friends. These people make up our inner circle, and they get more of our time. Then come work and friends. This approach helps us to prioritize what we do. It equips us to say yes to the people and events that are most important, as well as to say no or maybe later to things that can wait.

To keep our relationships healthy, we must manage our resources and make sure that our most important relationships are getting the most of our time and energy. One of the ways to do this is to identify the people who are in our inner circle (those who will receive the most of what we have to offer), and those who are in our outer circle (those we interact with, but who don't receive as much of our time and energy). Creating this balance is valuable to everyone.

We can bring greater awareness to our inner and outer circles by asking ourselves good questions. Are we scheduling time for God, our spouse and loved ones? Are we sending cards to those who live far from us, keeping those relationships alive? How are we keeping these relationships strong?

While the people in our lives need us, remember that our inner circle relationships need more of our consistent attention and energy so that they remain healthy. Our relationships take constant effort, which is why it is so important to be aware of our inner and outer circles and prioritizing our time and energy so that it goes where it is most needed. This consistent work on our part will bring great benefits to us and others.

In families, a wise way to evaluate is to consider first the truth about the needs between you and your spouse, as this relationship can provide balance to the whole household. Then, you may begin to consider your relationship with your children.

For example, are you taking time each day to pray with your spouse? Do you schedule a weekly date? Are you scheduling time to read to your children and pray with them each night? Loving others requires different things for different individuals. "Love" is a huge word—with so much nuance in it. This is why we need to seek God's wisdom and guidance in how to handle each of our relationships effectively and appropriately.

Consistency is so important—for example, we can't simply play with our child once and then expect that to be good enough to last them for months. They need daily, loving interactions. Our lives change and we need to constantly evaluate needs. When your children are grown, it will not be enough to call them once and then not call again for months. To keep the connection vibrant, we must speak with each other and be there for each other. We keep our relationships healthy through listening, encouraging, giving, spending time, offering emotional support, and being present.

As we've discussed already, our relationships take time and energy. And if we are not reviewing our schedule, and how much time is needed to make sure we are making time for God, restoring ourselves and discerning time with others, something will suffer. This is another reason to surround ourselves with people who encourage us to rest and receive what we need—spiritually, emotionally, physically, financially, and relationally. By doing so, we help ourselves stay balanced and healthy, and we avoid burnout.

As we learn to properly care for and balance our inner circle relationships, it becomes easier to know how much time and energy we have for our outer circle. All the while, we can remain aware of our own need for self-care and time with the Lord. Thus, we can be a blessing to others, without exhausting ourselves.

Great Communication Is Essential to Relationship Success

People are complicated. We each have multiple roles that we take on, depending on who we are in relationships with. For example, I am a wife, a mother, a mother-in-law, a daughter, a sister, a friend, a volunteer, a Christian life coach, a businesswoman and entrepreneur, an author, a churchgoer…and much more. And those in my sphere of influence also have many roles they play. They each have six areas of life that they are navigating, just as I am.

What this means is that we all have complex needs that are changing all the time as our lives ebb and flow. These complexities can make our relationships difficult unless we learn to communicate well and use what we are learning to foster stronger connections as we become aware of life's changes. The more we are aware of what is happening right now in our lives and the lives of those in our sphere of influence, the more we can be equipped to make good decisions to keep our relationships on track.

There are so many areas of communication available to us in the six key areas of our lives. We can use our awareness of these areas to our advantage as we take an interest in the lives of others and thus build rapport, making our relationships more successful and healthier. What is rapport? It is the ability to relate to another person, to find common ground and similar interests.

The very act of healthy communication begins with great questions so we can understand the other person and therefore create rapport. There are so many questions we can ask others to find out about their lives and offer positive words that will bless them. People do not care about how much you know until they know how much you care. When you show you care about people by fostering good, open, caring communication, it will deepen the relationship you have with them. (Asking great questions and developing rapport are topics that I explain in more detail in my book, *A Coach for Christ*, and in several of my resources and classes on www.LaVonneEarl.com.)

As we are relating to others, we can keep in mind that they may be hurting or in need. Listen for the message they are communicating to you, either openly or secretly. Ask yourself, "Where has this person been hurt? What do they need? What unmet desires do they have? How can I meet their needs?" Ask them open-ended questions, encourage them to share, and be willing to listen, paying attention to what they are saying, what they may be fearing, what they may be concerned about, and so on.

We can also call on the Lord to help us as we communicate. As Christians, we have the Holy Spirit living inside of us, ready to guide us. When we ask Him, He will tell us where others need encouragement, where they need a word that will edify them and strengthen them. He aids us in our communication with others when we allow Him. In this way, we will be a blessing. We'll be life-giving water to those around us.

As we take on a servant mentality, taking the other person into account, rapport will be more easily established. As you think about establishing rapport with someone, consider how to best approach the other person by finding common ground to create harmony. We may have the right intentions, yet still take the wrong approach. I've made that mistake myself. We all do. As we stay aware of where others are at, what their love language is, and what their needs are—as well as being more aware of ourselves—we can approach conversations in ways that build connection and unity. Our purpose should always be to find ways of helping others with the intent of demonstrating the love of Jesus.

Consider whether the person will be able to receive what you are saying with the approach you are taking. An example that we're all familiar with is how we handle conflict. Many times, people become angry and instead of processing how they can best approach the individual, they express their anger with yelling, blaming, and condemnation. How likely is it that the person on the receiving end will understand your needs and the conflict will be solved? Not very. That approach makes it harder for others to receive, rather than easier.

Know also that your silence speaks volumes! Those close to you should never have to guess whether you love them or not, or whether you are angry. The silent treatment can be very painful. Make sure you go the second mile as Jesus commanded. If someone asks you for something, be sure to respond, at least with encouragement. Be mindful of how people are starving for love and grace—and give freely!

In addition, keep in mind that some people may be better able to have hard conversations whereas others are not strong enough for difficult conversations. For those individuals, it is especially important to consider how to broach an important topic with greater gentleness for those who need it more.

Being mindful and aware of others, as well as all circumstances as you make good plans for communicating well with others, will likely make your conversations go more smoothly. It increases the likelihood you will create a win-win for all, thus strengthening and deepening your relationships.

We All Need Forgiveness

At times in our relationships, forgiveness may be needed—because mistakes are made, hurts happen, and we can wrong each other. Part of being aware of how well our relationships are going is to consider areas where we may need to ask forgiveness or offer forgiveness.

To be able to offer forgiveness to one who has hurt us, we must renew our minds and allow the Lord to bring healing into our lives. To ask for forgiveness, we must recognize and release any pride we may have about the situation where we have done wrong. Therefore, forgiveness can be a challenging task, but it can be made easier as we transform our thinking.

Yes, there are certainly thoughts that have a strong emotional component to them, especially if we have experienced something painful or traumatic. God created our minds to protect us. Therefore, your mind will often remind you when something awful happened. It is trying to keep you safe from this awful event so it will never happen again.

So, what if we could change our thoughts? God says that we can. He says ALL things are possible with Him! Even though our minds tend to remember the worst of things, we can still be in the driver's seat and dictate what we will think about! How then do we resolve the issue so we can bring peace back into our lives?

To balance healing and protection with forgiveness, we will need to examine our thoughts, apply God's Word, ask great questions, and make decisions that are good and godly. Always keep in mind that transformation begins with awareness. Before we can act, we must first be aware and clear on the truth.

If you have found yourself in a situation where wrongs have been committed, you might ask yourself: "What is true about what happened? Are there ways in which I am being prideful and unwilling to admit wrongdoing? Have I held onto hurt feelings and old wounds? Have I asked the Lord to bring healing to me, so that I may be able to forgive and move on?"

Know that asking these questions may take a while, and this is ok. We need time to process in our minds the tragedy that occurred, so do not feel that you must rush through it.

The next step would be to determine what it is you want to accomplish in your life. Is it gaining more peace? Forgetting about the event? The surest way to gain these things is to forgive. It removes the venom that is harming you.

What forgiveness means is that you are willing to surrender this toxic situation or person to the Lord for justice. You are removing the person and the situation from your thoughts and letting it go.

This is a very healthy place to be! In this way, you are creating room in your heart, mind, and life for good things. It is hard for good to come into your life when you are occupied with hurtful thoughts. Forgiveness sets you free for good to come in!

Please understand, though, that forgiveness does not mean reconciliation. It isn't always possible to reconcile with everyone, especially if the person you are forgiving is unsafe. Remember—you are valuable to the Lord, and He wants you safe and well. You may need to set some appropriate boundaries, which we'll discuss next.

Guarding Our Hearts and Setting Healthy Boundaries

Loving others can be complicated, but it doesn't need to be, as God will reveal to us through the 5 Keys (described in Week One) what the truth is in each relationship we have. Remember, there are appropriate boundaries we can benefit from in our relationships. Even the scriptures encourage us that there are times to *"avoid bad company"* (1 Corinthians 15:33) or *"shake the dust off our feet"* (Matthew 10:14).

Although we are to love our neighbors, we also must learn to discern when it is time to guard our hearts. Remember, we live in a broken world, with broken people. As a result, some relationships can be or become toxic. Some people may not be good influences for us as God intends. Instead, they may tear us down, or even cause us to sin. We must therefore be careful in choosing who we are close to, and who we are spending our time with.

We need to constantly evaluate all our relationships as well as renew our minds in order to remain well. In my coaching business, I often work with people who have ended a poor relationship, but the effects of that relationship have continued to live in their minds. This is not healthy, and our minds must be renewed so that we can be free from those lingering negative thought patterns that have hindered our success.

Fortunately, we can rely on God's wisdom to help us keep our love for others while setting healthy boundaries to protect ourselves and others as needed. As we seek the Holy Spirit for guidance, direction, and wisdom, He will guide us to the right choices for our relationships. Sometimes, that means creating greater space between oneself and a specific other person. At times, this is the most loving approach we can take!

From our vantage point as human beings, we can only judge others by their fruit. There may be a lot going on in their heart, including good motives and positive desires they may have. It may not all be negative. Yet we cannot know what is in their heart. We can only see what they are producing through their words and actions. So, that's how we determine the plans we make for how we will handle certain relationships.

Perhaps there are people in your past who did harm to you, and as a result there is trauma from what occurred. This is where setting firm boundaries in place can be freeing for you. Having worked with many people who have experienced trauma, I am a firm believer in boundaries. Boundaries help protect us so we can heal and move forward in the way that God intends.

Using the 5 Keys to Success in Our Relationships

As we navigate our relationships, we can follow the 5 Keys to Success—knowing the truth, setting a goal along with its purpose, planning, taking action steps and being held accountable, and being a blessing to others. (If you need a recap, we discussed these 5 keys in Week One: From Glory to Glory, and you can feel free to review that section before reading further here.) Using these 5 keys will help us gain understanding of where we are at right now in our relationships, discover what we'd like to change, and move toward the transformation we desire.

This transformation process begins with the truth. Every relationship we have has a different priority in our lives, and these priorities may even shift as the situations of life shift and change. How we make decisions will be based on the truth of their importance and the facts that are relevant in each situation.

Our relationships are important to our overall well-being. To be successful in them, we must be aware of what is happening in them. As Christian believers, we have been given the gift of the Holy Spirit to help us to recognize the truth about our relationships with God, ourselves, and others. We can then make good decisions for ourselves so we can move forward and be successful in our relationships.

Once you are aware of the truth, move onto the next steps in the 5 Keys. What goals do you want to set, and what is the purpose behind those goals? What actions will you take to achieve success? How will you keep yourself accountable in pursuing those actions? What will success look like to you?

Managing our relationships requires rapport, which involves listening to others, understanding them, and finding positive ways to relate. To develop rapport, we must be flexible and able to adapt to each situation and person according to their needs.

To begin, focus on praying and being led by the Holy Spirit as you discover what is true about your relationships. Ask God to show you what goals, plans and actions need to be in place to help you be transformed in this area of life.

Here is an example of one way this approach can be applied in everyday life.

Imagine that you have an individual in your life with special needs or wants. Many of us do, and it can be a challenging area to navigate. As you evaluate your situation with this person, you can begin by identifying the truth.

What is true about the people in your life and their needs? What is true about what they are capable of? What is true about you? Are you rested? Do you have the patience and energy you need to interact with the person in question? Perhaps the truth is that you have a headache today, and that may make you less patient. And perhaps that means it would be wise to take a nap and an aspirin before interacting with that person.

As you can see, knowing these things can help you decide how to interact with others each day, depending on what is happening with them and with you. And this awareness is something we can have daily in all our relationships. Things will shift and change as our lives ebb and flow.

Remember, I'm not saying we will not make mistakes. We will, because we are human and fallible, but as we remain aware, we will be more likely to notice our missteps more quickly. In this way, we can correct them and move forward. The more we become aware, the more opportunities we will have to be successful in our relationships.

Doing Your Best by Applying the 5 Keys

"Do your best to live as everybody's friend."
—**Romans 12:18 (TPT)**

In relationships, there are always two people involved. What happens depends on both individuals, not just one. There will be times that you are not able to achieve your goals fully because the other person may not be interested or capable of taking their action steps. But as much as it depends on you, do what you can to live in peace with them.

We can only do our best. We may have the perfect approach, yet that person may still receive something wrong. Relationships are complex! But we can turn to God for His guidance. As we walk in His will, according to the Bible and His guidance, we can then choose to do as He directs us. He will direct us as to the steps we must take, we can then be at peace, knowing we have done our part.

Doing your best in a relationship means applying the 5 Keys, seeking reconciliation when it is appropriate to do so, and letting go when it is time to move on.

For example, you may have a relationship that is broken, such as in the case of an imminent divorce or a dysfunctional family relationship that has led to estrangement. Perhaps you would like to see this relationship reconciled, if possible.

This is an understandable goal, but keep in mind that there is another person involved. You must therefore look at the truth of the situation. Does the other person desire to reconcile as well? If they do not, then your goal must change and adapt to what is true. Reconciliation is not possible if the other person does not wish to move toward that goal with you. In cases such as this, your goal needs to change to what is possible.

Again, you can ask yourself the truth about the situation and what you need to move forward. Perhaps the goal will change from reconciliation (which requires the other person's cooperation) to gaining peace of mind (which depends upon you and God, not the other person). Consider the purpose behind the goal. How will peace of mind benefit you? Will it help you to focus on what matters in your life, such as your child, your job, and your time with God? This is so beneficial, because it will help you to move forward and live productively, whether the other person wishes to end the estrangement or not.

During this process, you can apply the scripture that says to live in peace with others—as much as depends upon you. Perhaps your goal might be to live in peace with your divorced spouse or your estranged family member, being able to be kind with your words when you see them, rather than feeling angry and hurt. That is a goal that would bring you benefits, as you would feel peaceful, not agitated. This is an obtainable goal as it matches your purpose to feel peace.

At this point, you can determine a plan and the action steps related to it. What are you going to do with your relationship to get where you want to go? What will it take for you to experience peace in this situation?

Perhaps you will pray, confess peace over yourself, and read scriptures on peace every day. You might journal about your relationship or work through your feelings with a Christian coach or even a therapist. Maybe you will pay attention to the other areas of your life, acknowledging that when you feel tired or ill, you won't be at your best. At such times, you can limit your exposure to the person so that you limit your chances to become upset.

Building in accountability by having some trusted, godly people you can go to for support as you take your action steps is key. A life coach, pastor, godly friend, or counselor can serve this role for you.

And finally, when you are successfully able to walk in greater peace with this person, you can share your encouragement, prayers, and godly advice with others who are in the same situation you were once in. You can help others thrive who are going through a divorce, giving back what God has done for you.

When you know you have done your best in your relationships, then you can be confident in moving forward into what God has called you to do next. And this helps to bring balance to this entire area of your life.

Day 1

Relationships
Loving God and Others

"Jesus answered him, 'Love the Lord your God with every passion of your heart, with all the energy of your being, and with every thought that is within you.' This is the great and supreme commandment. And the second is like it in importance: 'You must love your friend in the same way you love yourself.'"
—**Matthew 22:36–39 (TPT)**

Since *"contained within these commandments to love you will find all the meaning of the Law and the Prophets"* (Matthew 22:40 TPT), this is an important scripture to memorize. In these scriptures, we are reminded that *love* is at the root of all our relationships with God and others. God Himself is Love (1 John 4:16), and to be His disciple is to be filled with that love and to be directed by it in all we do. As we let His love fill us and guide us, we'll know what to do in relation to God and people. Love does not mean ignoring wrongs or condoning sin, but instead responding to those around us in godly ways that draw them to repentance, forgiveness, and transformation in Him—which is His highest and best for us all.

Gain Insight

Answer the questions, be honest with yourself and be transformed!

1. How does God use you to express His love to people?

   _____
   _____
   _____

2. How does God use others to express His love to you?

   _____
   _____
   _____

3. How does loving yourself change the way you love others?

   _____
   _____
   _____

4. Can you love others even through separation?

   _____
   _____
   _____

5. What are some ways to love others when you must be apart?

   _____
   _____
   _____

Pray

Thank You, Lord, for Your love toward me. Help me to love you with every part of my being—heart, soul, and mind. Thank You for showing me how to love. Help me to be guided and directed by You as I love others.

Day 2

Relationships
Boundaries

*"Don't continue to team up with unbelievers in mismatched alliances,
for what partnership is there between righteousness and rebellion?
Who could mingle light with darkness?"*
—**2 Corinthians 6:14 (TPT)**

I love this verse because it is such a powerful reminder that setting boundaries is healthy and something that God desires for us. Boundaries are not hateful rejections of others, but rather they are guides that we set around our own lives to help us to know and act on what is good and godly. Saying no to some things frees us up to say yes to other things. This is so valuable, because it helps us to walk out our purpose and plans in ways that honor the Lord. And boundaries help to keep us and others safe, so that God's will can be done in our lives and theirs.

Gain Insight

Answer the questions, be honest with yourself and be transformed!

1. Should your time, money and heart be given to everyone?

2. What type of people should you avoid?

3. Who are your closest relationships?

4. Who gets first priority of your time, money and heart? Second priority? Third?

5. Is it of God to have healthy, godly people closest to you? For what reason?

Pray

Lord, thank You for guiding me to the good and godly people in my life. Help me to be wise and discerning about who I allow to get close to me. Strengthen me spiritually, Lord, so I hear Your voice and recognize truth. Don't allow the enemy to give me guilt for setting healthy boundaries so I can follow through on what you direct me to do. Help me to be kind in my boundaries and still love even when setting myself apart for Your glory.

Day 3

Relationships
Godly Communication

"And never let ugly or hateful words come from your mouth, but instead let your words become beautiful gifts that encourage others; do this by speaking words of grace to help them."
—**Ephesians 4:29 (TPT)**

How we speak to one another has such a powerful impact on the health, strength and well-being of our relationships. In this area, we can let God be our guide. What would He say to others if He stood in our shoes? After all, He is within us because we are His children and His disciples. So, we are to be His representative in how we communicate—which includes our choice of words, our tone of voice, our willingness to listen as well as talk, our genuine interest in others, and a heart to create goodness, grace and light as a result of our communications with those around us.

Gain Insight

Answer the questions, be honest with yourself and be transformed!

1. Are you speaking to others the way God intends?

   _____
   _____
   _____

2. What needs to be improved?

   _____
   _____
   _____

3. When others are unkind, are you able to kindly set healthy boundaries?

4. Do you complain easily?

5. Do you listen well?

Pray

Lord, help me to communicate with others in a godly way. Help me to bless others even if they curse me. Help me to be an example of Your love. Help me to listen more than I speak. Help me to see the good in my life and how I am blessed so that I don't complain.

Day 4

Relationships
Good Company

"So stop fooling yourselves!
Evil companions will corrupt good morals and character."
—1 Corinthians 15:33 (TPT)

The people we are connected with have such a strong influence on us. They can build us up and encourage us to move into greater successes, or they can tear us down and discourage us, so that we begin to think we are incapable of achieving what God has put in our heart to do for Him. This doesn't mean that we do not interact with unbelievers, but rather we are to carefully consider our relationships and keep them balanced. We can spend more time with those who uplift us in the Lord, and set boundaries with those who provoke us into sin, bad behavior, negativity and other ways of living that do harm to us.

Gain Insight

Answer the questions, be honest with yourself and be transformed!

1. What if a family member is considered "bad company?"

2. Are lazy people a good influence?

3. Are there angry people within your sphere of influence? What can you do?

4. Greedy people constantly take. Would this be considered a healthy relationship?

5. Are there any sinful people within your sphere of influence?

Pray

Lord, thank You for guiding and directing me to safe and good people to do life with. Help me to be wise in my choice of friendships. Help me to be kind while also keeping healthy boundaries. Keep me from any guilt for protecting my body, mind, and spirit and to know that boundaries are from You.

Day 5

Relationships
Forgiveness

*"But if we freely admit our sins when his light uncovers them,
he will be faithful to forgive us every time. God is just to forgive us our sins
because of Christ, and he will continue to cleanse us from all unrighteousness."*
—1 John 1:9 (TPT)

*"But if you withhold forgiveness from others,
your Father withholds forgiveness from you."*
—Matthew 6:15 (TPT)

As humans living in a fallen world, we all have flaws. We make mistakes. We can hurt others, and others may hurt us. Learning to navigate these issues means learning to forgive. Think of forgiveness as being similar to releasing a debt. You can decide that the person no longer "owes" anything to you. This frees you to have energy for things that are productive in your life. Remember, forgiveness is for our good—yet it doesn't mean you have to permit the wrong to happen again. Rather, you set boundaries to help yourself walk in forgiveness while also keeping yourself in a safe and healthy position.

Gain Insight

Answer the questions, be honest with yourself and be transformed!

1. What difference does it make in your life to know that God forgives you?

2. Is there anyone you need to forgive?

3. Do you believe you can forgive and not reconcile with another person?

4. What factor does trust play in reconciliation?

5. What are some steps you can take to help you to forgive both yourself and others?

Pray

Lord, thank You for Your forgiveness toward me. I am so grateful for all that You do for me. Help me to forgive others their trespasses. Help me to use wisdom when reconciling with others. Help me to live at peace with all people so long as it depends on me. Help me to set boundaries in love.

Day 6

Relationships
Reconciliation

"And God has made all things new, and reconciled us to himself,
and given us the ministry of reconciling others to God."
—**2 Corinthians 5:18 (TPT)**

The greatest reconciliation that has ever happened in history is the work that Jesus has done on the Cross. By paying for our sin and taking our place of punishment, He paved the way for us to be brought back into a healthy, loving relationship with God. Reconciliation is a two-way street—God has done His part by forgiving us and inviting us back into relationship; we must do our part by repenting, turning to Him, and giving Him the opportunity to transform our lives.

Likewise, in our relationship with other people, there will be times when wrongs are done. Forgiveness must take place, and then if both parties are willing to repent and work toward transformation, we can potentially begin to come back into a healthy, loving relationship. Reconciliation, therefore, is a process that takes time so that trust can be rebuilt and healthy patterns of interacting can be established.

Gain Insight

Answer the questions, be honest with yourself and be transformed!

1. How has God reconciled you to Himself?

   _____
   _____
   _____

2. While in a relationship with God, is it important for you to repent when you sin?

   _____
   _____
   _____

3. What does it mean to be reconciled to others?

4. What kind of people can we be reconciled with?

5. What is your part in helping others be reconciled to God?

Pray

Thank You, Lord Jesus, that You choose to be in a relationship with me. Help me to continually give to You in our relationship as I know You continually give to me. Help me to be wise in who I reconcile with here on earth. I know I can extend love and blessings without being in a relationship with those unwilling to change for good. Help me to be a good influence and to point others to You, so they can be reconciled with You. I know it is only in a relationship with You that anyone can have true hope for their life.

Day 7

Relationships
Rest

"Are you weary, carrying a heavy burden? Come to me. I will refresh your life, for I am your oasis. Learn my ways and you'll discover that I'm gentle, humble, and easy to please. You will find refreshment and rest in me. For all that I require of you will be pleasant and easy to bear."
—**Matthew 11:28–30 (TPT)**

Relationships are not meant to constantly drain us and tear us down. There is to be give and take so that we can have balance in our lives. A healthy relationship can even be restorative, as we can provide each other with encouragement, kind words, and strength in times of need. Beyond that, taking time to rest is a great way to restore our energy, which then helps us to be our best selves in our relationships. A good balance of time with others who uplift us, and time for self-care, can do so much good for all our relationships.

Gain Insight

Answer the questions, be honest with yourself and be transformed!

1. Will healthy relationships encourage you to rest?

2. How does Jesus reflect a healthy relationship?

3. Does having the right people in your life bring peace?

4. How do your relationships benefit when you rest?

5. Do healthy people push you to extremes?

Pray

Thank You, Lord, that You give me rest. Thank You for the peace You bring to me. Help me seek those who also walk in Your peace and rest. Help me to be wise in the work that I choose, the friends that I choose, and any activity that I choose to engage in. Let all that I do be for Your glory and my good.

Week Three: Relationships

Reflection for the Week on Relationships

Answer the questions, be honest with yourself and be transformed!

1. Are you moving closer to your relationship goals?

2. Is there anything getting in the way?

3. Do you need to set any new plans?

4. Have you found an accountability partner?

5. In what ways can you help someone in their relationship life?

Write Your Inner Narration

Using what you have learned from this chapter, the scriptures you have memorized this week, and what you discovered while answering this week's questions, build on your original narration from weeks 1 and 2, and write an additional short godly narration using only positive words. If you find it helpful, review your answers to the daily questions from this week, take note of any positive words, and include them in your new godly narration for this week.

Example: I AM beautiful. I AM loved by God, just as I AM.
I AM forgiven. I AM pleasing to God. I AM strong. I AM courageous.

I AM filled with godly purpose. I AM equipped and able to achieve my godly goals.
I AM a son or a daughter of the King. I AM covered in His grace.
Nothing anyone says or does can harm me because I AM protected.

I AM healthy in my boundaries. I AM forgiving. I AM loved in my relationships.
I AM wise and gracious in my interactions with others in my life, etc.

Week Four

Emotional Wellness

Have you ever felt like your emotions were so out of control that you were going to lose your mind? Or, like your emotions were not working for your benefit and you wonder where the joy in life is at? Perhaps you've felt as if fear was going to overtake you, or that anger and worry are your constant companions, making it difficult to relax and experience times of peace and joy. Or perhaps you struggle to express your emotions in a healthy way that benefits you and others around you. Maybe you even have trouble identifying how you feel when something happens that is not ideal.

If you don't know what you are feeling, it can be hard to discern the right actions to take to improve your life. And if your emotions are taking you over and driving you to make poor choices, the results can be a life that is filled with difficulties. You're not alone—many people struggle with their feelings, which is what makes gaining emotional well-being such a valuable area to pursue.

As we look at the world we live in, it becomes clear that the need for emotional wellness is essential for all people. There's so much fear in our world, so much anger, so much emotional instability. We can see it all around us. These are incredibly difficult times that we are living in right now. There is a lot of confusion about the situations we find ourselves facing, and things that most of us do not agree with happen every day.

In addition, many of us grew up in families that were dysfunctional in how emotions were expressed. Some families encouraged the idea of stuffing down emotional responses; therefore, we didn't gain the skills to recognize what we are feeling and how to act on them in healthy ways. Other families had a "let it all hang out" approach, where emotions were constantly high and constantly expressed. Without a sense of proper balance, our emotional displays can cause much pain and harm, both to ourselves and others.

Additionally, you may have personal stress that you are going through, such as job loss, divorce, lack, isolation, illness, and other stressors. It then becomes natural to wonder how one can have a sound mind and emotionally stable soul in times like these.

For you, I have good news! God desires all of us to have emotional wholeness, well-being, and stability, so that we can be blessed and also so that we can be a refuge for others to run to when their world is being shaken. As believers, we are to gain the necessary skills to care for ourselves body, mind and spirit to keep our emotional health at its very best.

God is not surprised by any of the things happening in our world. He is our anchor, our Rock, and He desires for us to be healthy and whole as we go through such a time as this. God has not left us without a plan to be emotionally well and complete.

The Value of a Healthy Soul

"Beloved friend, I pray that you are prospering in every way and that you continually enjoy good health, just as your soul is prospering."
—1 John 3:2 (TPT)

The Bible talks often about the soul, and so do human beings—inside and outside of church, in all sorts of settings. But what does that word *soul* mean? Many Christian theologians make a distinction between the *spirit* (the part of us that is connected to God and made in His image), and the *soul*—the part of us that is uniquely us, meaning our mind, our will, and yes, our emotions.

So, as you consider the verse above, you might read it this way: "I pray that you are prospering in every way, *just as your mind, your will, and your emotions are prospering*." In other words, God desires you to be doing well in your emotional life, because it is an essential part of your being. God doesn't look at emotions as bad, as sinful in themselves, as something to be avoided. But like every other gift He has given us, He desires for us to learn how to properly use our emotions.

Your emotional life is a part of you that can be balanced and healthy. Emotions are not meant to be feared or avoided, but they are to be effectively managed so that we can be our best selves in Christ. Rather than being led by our emotions and acting on them without thinking, we can learn and gain skills that help us to act wisely when it comes to how we are feeling at a given moment in time.

As we gain the skills to manage our emotional life, we'll find ourselves able to handle any emotional situation. You learn to step back, breathe, recognize what you are feeling, and turn to the Lord in prayer to seek His guidance, instead of simply acting in the moment. The ability to recognize that feelings change, together with the knowledge that we do have *many* courses of action we can take in response to our feelings, allows us the ability to make good choices that benefit us and those around us.

I encourage you to take to heart what this verse tells us about our well-being. As we learn how to do well in our emotions, then our soul, meaning the other areas of our life, will prosper too! Having our soul healed will help us to continue to prosper, be successful, and have great health, balance and well-being in every area of our life, including our emotions.

Our own healing is so vital because from the place of healing, we can heal others. Hurt people hurt people, but loved people love people, and healed people heal people. Whatever is occurring in our life that is causing emotional distress, we need to get that area healed and well, so that we can have emotional wellness, enjoy a more balanced life, and live out our godly purpose for His glory. That is God's best for you!

Gaining a Sound Mind in Stressful Times

The Bible makes it clear that God desires us to enjoy soundness—balance, health, and well-being in our emotional life. What is especially amazing is how this promise comes to us through the apostle Paul during one of his most challenging moments.

Imagine the great stress that Paul and the rest of the disciples were going through as they shared the good news about Jesus in their day. Their safety was often at stake as they would preach the Gospel. They were threatened by both the religious leaders and the governmental leaders of their day, who didn't want their way of life to be disrupted by the preaching of the Gospel.

One of the worst persecutors of Christians in Paul's day was the Emperor Nero. As the leader of Rome, Nero was determined to kill Christians. He had them arrested, impaled on stakes, and lit on fire.

During this period of great struggle, danger and stress, Paul was put in prison for preaching the Gospel. Yet even in that difficult experience, Paul was led to write to the Christian churches where he had often ministered and shared God's Word. Inspired by the Holy Spirit, he offered great empowerment to Christians throughout the ages to come when he imparted to his ministry partner, Timothy, God's Word in a letter.

> *"For God will never give you the spirit of fear, but the Holy Spirit*
> *who gives you mighty power, love, and **self-control**."*
> —**2 Timothy 1:7 (TPT)**

Self-control is about choosing to allow the Holy Spirit to empower you and give you soundness of mind, or the peace of God that passes all understanding. The New King James translation says it like this:

> *"For God has not given us a spirit of fear,*
> *but of power and of love and a **sound mind**."*
> —**2 Timothy 1:7 (NKJV)**

Through these inspired words, Paul encouraged Timothy to rely on what God had given him to fulfill his purpose—power, love, and soundness of mind, which includes healthy emotions in the face of hardships. Paul knew—and God knew—that Timothy would need more strength and soundness of mind as he continued in his calling as a Christian to spread the Good News of the Gospel.

The phrase *sound mind* is taken from the Greek word *sophroneo*, which is a compound word. This first part comes from the word *sozo*, which means *to be saved, delivered, rescued, revived, salvaged, and protected*. The individual is now safe and secure. It's like a person who is on the verge of death but then is revived and resuscitated because new life has been breathed into him.

The second part of the phrase *sound mind* refers to *intelligence or total frame of thinking, including rationale, logic, and emotions*. The word *phroneo* refers to *every part of the human mind*, including all the processes that are engaged in making the mind function and come to conclusions.

Taken together, *sound mind* describes a mind that is rescued, revived, protected and now safe and secure. Knowing that we are secure and provided for by God is essential to helping us find balance when our emotions are in flux. And we can lean on God to protect our mind and shield our thoughts from the lies of the devil. Anytime you are tempted to succumb to fear, anger, hurt, or other painful emotions, you can allow God's Word and the Holy Spirit to work in you to deliver, rescue, and revive you.

Press into the goodness of God and His love for you. Turn to Him, and trust Him with your whole heart, mind, and soul. By doing so daily, you will receive the sound mind that God has given to you!

Finding Balance in Our Emotions

To do well in life, God says that our soul needs to prosper. But how do we bring about a prosperous, healthy soul—with a healthy mind and emotions?

I believe one way to look at this question is to understand what God's best for us is when it comes to our emotional life. It's important to realize that emotions are not automatically bad; it is how we handle them that is key to our well-being. Emotions themselves are given to us for our benefit; they can teach us to be aware of what is going on around us and within us, so that we can use that information to make good decisions.

But because we live in a fallen world, we often find ourselves surrounded by situations that can cause emotions that trouble us, such as stress and worry, rather than peace. Often, these emotions can seem out of our control. They may even cause us to think that we are stuck with negative feelings forever. But remember, our emotions shift and change. We have more control over our emotional life than the world and our family of origin may have led us to believe.

Rather than being trapped by our emotions, we can learn to recognize them. We can become aware of what they are telling us, and then make good decisions that will bring about good for us. And as we do that, our emotions will shift!

Handling Worry with God's Word

One of the most common areas of emotional distress for people is "worry." Worry is *mental distress*, primarily over a negative possibility in the future. It is a state of mind, a way of thinking, a mental habit—a preoccupation with something bad that may happen. When worry fills our mind, the Bible tells us that it leads to emotional pain: *"My thoughts trouble me, and I am distraught"* (Psalm 55:2 NIV).

Jesus says, *"The worries of this life…come in and choke the Word, making it unfruitful"* (Mark 4:19 NIV). Worry divides the mind between what is motivating and demotivating, what is constructive and destructive. James chapter 1 tells us that a double-minded man will fall. Therefore, to experience emotional wellness, one step we must take is to transform our habits to get rid of the "what-if thinking" that doesn't serve us well.

To help us stand against worry and distressing thoughts, God has provided a solution for us—His perfect peace! Isaiah 26:3 (NIV) speaks of God's will for our minds: *"You will keep in perfect peace those whose minds are steadfast, because they trust in you."* The phrase *perfect peace* is the Hebrew word *shalom*, which means *wholeness, completeness, lacking in nothing*.

God has also given us instructions in His Word to make time for a sabbath each week—a peaceful time of rest for our body, mind, and spirit. Proper rest is a vital part of maintaining our emotional well-being! His plan is for us to find the restoration we need on a regular basis, even daily, so that we can experience a balanced, healthy emotional life.

Focusing on God and making time for Him in prayer, meditating on His Word, and worshipping Him will connect us to all the good things He has ordained for us. We can draw upon His comfort, His wisdom, His strength, and the other heavenly resources He makes available to us because we are born again. He is the Source of our stability, our Rock that gives us a firm foundation to stand on in an ever-changing world. This can bring us great peace and calm in our emotions.

Developing an Attitude of Hope

Another common emotional state that gives many people trouble is discouragement and doubt. We live in a fallen world and things are known to let us down; it is easy for us to default to a negative outlook on life. If we then begin to expect bad things to happen, our emotions will follow suit, and we may find ourselves feeling unhappy, down, resentful, and even depressed. These feelings often arise when we feel we do not have control of our life.

But I have good news! God has not set us up to fail. He desires us to be more than conquerors, victorious in our life, and that includes our emotional well-being. He has a solution for our feelings of discouragement and lack of control. And it starts with godly hope.

Think of hope as having godly vision for your life. It is the act and state of visualizing the promises of God. As we focus on who we are in Christ, and what we have been called to accomplish as His disciples, we can be encouraged that we have so much to look forward to in our life! Jesus Himself anchors us so that we can have hope of good things to come.

> *"We have this certain hope like a strong,*
> *unbreakable anchor holding our souls to God himself.*
> *Our anchor of hope is fastened to the mercy seat in the heavenly realm*
> *beyond the sacred threshold, and where Jesus, our forerunner, has gone in before us.*
> *He is now and forever our royal Priest like Melchizedek."*
> **—Hebrews 6:19–20 (TPT)**

The hope we have in Jesus—the promise of great things to come—is an anchor for the soul, firm and secure. This hope gives us a firm foundation that helps us to stand strong and rooted, even as the situations around us cause us to experience a range of changing emotions.

Here's more good news: You weren't created to carry heavy burdens. It isn't God's will for your mind to be glued to your problems. It's time—right now, today—to live with faith-filled expectation! It is time to stop rehearsing every negative detail of life. That habit stirs up negative feelings and negative thinking, and it is not productive. It does not help you to be well in body, mind and spirit.

Instead, lean on all the promises of God. Anchor yourself in the hope His Word contains for you. Begin to fully trust Him—and begin to notice how an attitude of trust and faith can relieve your negative feelings and help you to shift into a better sense of emotional balance.

Jesus paid the price to free you, but you must do your part. Shake off the heaviness. It's nothing more than a weighty lie. Exchange negativity for peace and joy by reminding yourself of the good. No matter how hard things are, there's always something to be thankful for. So today, create a list of your blessings and bring your attention back to the One who loves you.

Give yourself permission to trust God and to draw near to Him in prayer, praise, and worship. Enjoy time with Him. Allow Him to give you the sound mind, the peace, the hope, the joy, the calm no matter what. Remind yourself that you have His Holy Spirit living inside of you! You are a powerful creation made in the image of God! The same spirit who raised Jesus from the dead lives inside of you! You have nothing to fear! Live boldly and courageously with the sound mind Christ has given to you!

Practice Good Self-Care

How do we live with a sound mind? It begins with our habits. Building up your emotional well-being is rooted in the daily habits we create. As we take time to care for every area of our life, it will be much easier to work through our changing emotions and find ways to encourage ourselves daily.

There are so many ways that habits of good self-care can help us be emotionally healthy. First, I encourage you to take time to enjoy the outdoors. God has created a beautiful world for us to enjoy. He made beautiful flowers, a gorgeous sun, snow, rain, rainbows, trees…and all the other elements of the natural world that can support our emotional wellness. It is amazing how taking time to be in nature, go for a walk, and breathe fresh air can support how we feel and think.

Another way to support your emotional health is to get good rest. God created the world in six days, but on the seventh, He didn't keep creating. Instead, He rested and enjoyed what He had created. And He has instructed us to rest too. Taking time to relax, which includes getting plenty of restful sleep, is so important to our physical well-being and our emotional well-being too.

And there are many other ways you can offer yourself kind, loving care—such as receiving a manicure, taking a warm bath, taking a hike in the woods, eating a healthy meal, and much more. For example, healthy eating habits are good for our physical well-being, and they also support our emotional wellness because our bodies feel better when we eat what is good for us.

Taking time for fun activities with good friends can build us up as well. We are created to explore, to learn, to grow, and to be in fellowship with one another. As we make time for these activities in healthy ways, the negative thoughts, worries, and discouragement begin to lift, and we find ourselves making room for joy, laughter, and hope.

In deciding how to practice good self-care, remember YKI — You Know It. You know what is best for you because God lives within you, and if you will ask Him what you can do to support your emotional wellness, He will reveal it to you. The key is to ensure you are making time for these healing activities that help restore your soul and bring you balance in your emotions.

Take Time for Your Spiritual Life

All the areas of life overlap, which means that as we make room for tending to our spiritual well-being, that effort will help us to be well in our emotions too. Taking time for spiritual activities such as prayer will help you feel more emotionally balanced.

Many people I work with are new Christians who are just learning what it means to pray. If that's you, then let me encourage you to pray in a positive, faith-filled way, as your prayers will cause you to be transformed. God desires you to speak in faith and to encourage yourself by focusing on His promises and all the good He has for you during prayer.

When you pray, speak as though what you are asking for has already happened. This is faith! Speak as if you are already healed, expressing your gratitude for what Jesus has already accomplished for you on the Cross.

If this sounds new to you, let me assure you it is simple. Here's an example that you can pray right now over yourself:

"Thank You, Lord, that I AM an overcomer, that I AM well and whole, that I AM filled with the peace of God that passes all understanding and guards my heart and mind in Christ!"

Do you see how that prayer focuses on what God says is true about you? You don't have to ask for what He has already given you, but you can agree with it! Really focus on gratitude and speak as though things have already happened. This will help you be emotionally well.

Another way to build yourself up emotionally is to sing and praise the Lord. The more we praise and worship and rejoice in the Lord, the happier we become. The act of praise and worship brings us joy and peace, and it invites the Lord to be present with us. His presence is so essential to our emotional well-being. Remember, too, that praise and worship is something we can do every day, not just on Sundays at church. Keep a song in your heart.

Walk in Your Purpose

Our joy is tied closely to our purpose. When we are not fulfilling our godly purpose, we will not be emotionally well. There is a space in our life that only God can fill. If you are not following your purpose—or perhaps are unsure what it is—then take the time to discover and pursue it, as this will be beneficial to your journey into greater emotional wellness.

There are many reasons that people may struggle in the area of purpose, and one of the most common ones is that we have not healed from painful past experiences. Often, I work with people who have gone through great pain in their life, and they have remained tied to the emotions related to their past experiences. And really, we all experience painful situations, some more than others, but nobody escapes having some pain in their lifetime. If you choose to wallow in your pain, it will keep you from the emotional well-being God desires for you to have.

If you have been through a traumatic event, seek the Lord's complete healing power so you can process what happened, including your emotions around that event. This makes it possible to move forward so you can be victorious, as God created you to be. I teach a course called *Born to Bloom*, for those who have experienced the trauma of sexual abuse. If that's you, please connect with me at www.LaVonneEarl.com/BorntoBloom.

How do we get free of the pain and move forward? First, we must stop asking why the pain happened. Begin instead asking, "What purpose can I achieve through this pain? Who can I help? How can I use this pain to bless other people? Who needs to hear about the good news of Jesus Christ, who heals us of pain?" Finding purpose in the pain you've gone through will bring you hope and healing. As you bless other people, this brings emotional wellness.

Even if things have been tremendously painful, you can make good choices about how you will interact with that pain. You can process it and use it to bless others, or you can choose self-pity. But self-pity will not bring you balance and well-being. Yes, take the time to process what you have been through, but look for ways to turn it for good as well.

Too often, we can take the trauma that has happened in our lives and focus only on that. But in Christ, we can stand back and, through His eyes, see the bigger picture. Begin looking at the grander, big God story of your life. Look for your purpose and find ways to serve others. As you do so, you will become the influential leader God has created you to be.

Stop focusing so much on yourself and what you have been through. Though you may be worried about what others think, most people are not going to judge you for what you have been through, where you've been and what you've done. They are looking to see how you are doing now, and what you are doing that is purpose-driven. They want to see you well and whole, and they will draw inspiration and encouragement from it for their own lives.

Focus on God, your purpose, and others. Take what He has given you and reach out to bless others! We are to become like Christ so that we can bring His glory to others, serve them, and help them gain what is good and true. Helping others be successful will bring us success too, and it will help us to experience joy, peace, and emotional wellness.

The Overlap between Relationships and Our Emotions

In my years of ministering through YKI coaching, I've come to see that the main reason people aren't doing well emotionally is that they have relationship challenges. When those issues aren't effectively addressed, they spill over into our emotions, causing disruptions there as well. As you know by reading this book, all these areas overlap and affect one another. Therefore, it is vital to address all of them and grow stronger and healthier in every area to create the balanced life God has intended for us to enjoy.

Notice that there are three main ways that our relationships can begin to negatively impact our emotional life.

First, we can become too focused on a relationship that is not going well. The issues in that relationship can draw too much of our thoughts, time, and energy. Perhaps we begin thinking only about what's going wrong. Or we stay too focused on an offense that was given, and the hurt we're feeling as a result. This excessive amount of attention can create a cascade of negativity and upset feelings, and it can become an obstacle to our emotional well-being.

Second, we may not be fully connected with or focused enough on the single most important relationship we'll ever have—our relationship with our Lord and Savior, Jesus Christ. Remember, all the issues of life flow out of the well-springs of our heart, which is the center of our relationship with God. This means that as we focus on Him and take the necessary time to feed our spirits with His Word, prayer, worship, and meditating on His truths, we can take the good fruit of that time into every other area of life. This centers us and gives us valuable peace and joy in Him, keeping our emotions stable day to day—something that is hard to maintain when we are not connected to God, as He is nourishment for our soul.

Third, we may not truly grasp who we are in Christ. When we don't know who we are in Him, it affects our relationship with our true self. This can create many different problems in how we relate to others, and how we think about ourselves—both of which can drain us and cause us to become weary.

Stay Connected

Relationships are so important to our emotional health. People who are struggling in their emotional life often are isolated or are connected to those who don't provide good support. The enemy would like nothing better than to keep us isolated and surrounded by negativity and lies.

God desires better for you! He has a plan to help you be emotionally well, and good, solid, healthy relationships are part of that plan.

Matthew 18:20 (TPT) says, *"For wherever two or three come together in honor of my name, I am right there with them!"*

Hebrews 10:25 (TPT) says, *"This is not the time to pull away and neglect meeting together, as some have formed the habit of doing. In fact, we should come together even more frequently, eager to encourage and urge each other onward as we anticipate that day dawning."*

When we are among other believers, it creates an atmosphere in which Jesus can come in and empower us and minister to us. As we gather with those who are spiritually minded, it is easier to find encouragement through God's Word, His Spirit, and worship.

Rather than isolating yourself, look for people who are safe, trustworthy, and committed to building you up. Stay connected with those who encourage you, keep you accountable, pray for you, and point you to God's Word and His goodness. Get involved in church, take time for godly fellowship, and pray with other believers. This is a biblical principle that God has given us for our emotional good.

Establishing Healthy Boundaries

Healthy boundaries help us to heal, because they create an environment where we can choose what is best for us at a given time. And choosing what is best for us supports our healing process.

Sometimes, these healthy boundaries need to be set around ourselves and our personal choices. For example, a person might have a tendency to turn to substances like drugs or alcohol when they are feeling emotionally vulnerable or distressed. Yet these substances do not promote healing. In this case, it may be necessary for the person to make choices that help them abstain, such as not bringing alcohol into their home. It may also mean choosing not to spend time with friends in places where the substance can easily be abused, such as bars.

There may be other times when healthy boundaries must be set into place between you and another person who is unsafe to be around. I teach a class that ministers to those who have been abused, and there are times that they must decide to put safe distance between themselves and the abuser, so that they can heal.

When it comes to emotions, we often need to set healthy boundaries regarding how we think about ourselves. Many of us learn to think negatively about ourselves, and when we are feeling emotionally vulnerable, those negative thoughts can run wild.

Using godly anchoring, I AM statements, and our godly narrations can all help us to redirect those thoughts onto what is good and true about us in Christ. And we can use those tools to support us as we set good boundaries around our thought life, refusing to dwell on what is not good for us, which allows us to find emotional balance and wellness.

What is wonderful about walking with God is that He will show us what we need to know in order to be emotionally whole and free. As you work on emotional wellness in your life, know that you can turn to the Lord in prayer, and ask Him for His help!

As you assess where you are at right now in your emotional wellness, you can make use of the 5 Keys to Success—our helpful process for evaluating our lives and making the decisions that will move us forward into a more balanced life in Christ. Begin to consider your emotional health by first discerning what is true about this area of your life.

As you work through this process, ask the Lord what you need to know about your emotions. Invite Him prayerfully to show you what you need to realize about the people and situations that are impacting your emotional life. As you seek the Lord, He will show you areas to focus on and what needs to be done for your healing.

Pray: "Lord, reveal to me anything in my life that I need to eliminate to be emotionally well." Expect Him to show you what needs to change to see progress in this area of your life.

Week Four: Emotional Wellness

Day 1

Emotional Wellness
The Peaceful, Abundant Life through Christ

*"The thief comes only to steal and kill and destroy;
I have come that they may have life, and have it to the full."*
—**John 10:10 (NIV)**

What a wonderful, encouraging verse of scripture this is! Jesus came not only to give us life, but to give us a life that is rich with joy, provision, abundance, grace, and every other good and godly thing you can imagine. He has come to *"give you everything in abundance, more than you expect—life in its fullness until you overflow"* (John 10:10 TPT). When we are full of the life He has for us, we'll find that we have plenty of what we need for our emotional wellness, including great peace of mind!

Gain Insight

Answer the questions, be honest with yourself and be transformed!

1. In what ways does the enemy try to steal your emotional wellness?

2. How does coming to the Lord cause you to be emotionally well?

3. Are you aware that your emotions shift and change?

4. What are your emotional wellness goals?

   _____

   _____

   _____

5. What steps can you take to achieve those goals?

   _____

   _____

   _____

Pray

Thank You, Lord, that You have come to give me life to the fullest! Help me to be aware of my emotions and take the steps necessary to be emotionally grounded in You. Transform me, Jesus, into Your likeness, centered on Your love and Your goodness. Give me daily internal joy so that I will experience great emotional health.

Week Four: Emotional Wellness

Day 2

Emotional Wellness
Meditation

*"So may the words of my mouth, my meditation-thoughts,
and every movement of my heart be always pure and pleasing,
acceptable before your eyes, Yahweh,
my only Redeemer, my Protector."*
—Psalm 19:14 (TPT)

*"Your magnificent splendor and the miracles of your majesty
are my constant meditation."*
—Psalm 145:5 (TPT)

Our thoughts are so key to what we feel at any given moment. And our emotions can have such an impact on how we think. If we are not careful, we can allow shifting emotions and thoughts to run away with us, causing us great distress. Fortunately, the Lord has given us the ability to choose what we think. The more we have His scriptures in our hearts and in front of us in our times of Bible study, the easier we make it for ourselves to notice thoughts that do not serve us, redirect our thinking to what He says about us, and tap into His peace.

Gain Insight

Answer the questions, be honest with yourself and be transformed!

1. What do your thoughts have to do with the way you feel?

2. What is your vision for today? For your future?

3. What meditation goals do you have?

4. In what ways will you speak life over yourself?

5. How much time do you spend praising the Lord and remembering His goodness daily?

Pray

Lord, bring to my mind all the miracles You have done for me. Thank You for all You have done for me. Lord, I will praise and worship You daily. You are such a good God! You have saved and delivered me! I know that You have great plans for me. Give me godly vision for my day and for my future. Thank You, Lord, for all that You have done for me!

Day 3

Emotional Wellness
Relationships

"So then, make it your top priority to live a life of peace with harmony in your relationships, eagerly seeking to strengthen and encourage one another."
—**Romans 14:19 (TPT)**

"You kissed my heart with forgiveness, in spite of all I've done. You've healed me inside and out from every disease."
—**Psalm 103:3 (TPT)**

Our relationships have such an impact on our emotional well-being that we cannot afford to ignore them. When we notice ourselves facing feelings of frustration, anger, fear, and negativity, one way to regain our emotional balance is to notice what is happening in our relationships. Often, old wounds that we have held onto can create unhealthy patterns that stand in the way of our emotional wellness. Thank God, He desires to bring us healing in those areas, so that we can walk in great peace with others, which is so good for our overall well-being.

Gain Insight

Answer the questions, be honest with yourself and be transformed!

1. How does keeping the peace with others affect your emotional health?

2. How do wounds from the past keep you from living peacefully with others?

3. What steps can you take to heal those wounds?

4. How does unforgiveness keep you from being emotionally well?

5. How does sharing the good news of the Gospel increase your emotional health?

Pray

Lord, help me to live at peace with everyone. Give me the courage and strength to forgive others and to heal. Keep me wise as I navigate difficult and toxic relationships. Help me to avoid anything that would steal my peace as I send loving thoughts and prayers their way.

Day 4

Emotional Wellness
Creation Brings Peace from the Creator

"Yahweh, our Sovereign God, your glory streams from the heavens above,
filling the earth with the majesty of your name! People everywhere see your splendor.
Look at the splendor of your skies, your creative genius glowing in the heavens.
When I gaze at your moon and your stars, mounted like jewels in their settings,
I know you are the fascinating artist who fashioned it all."
—**Psalm 8:1,3 (TPT)**

Have you ever noticed how taking time to sit outside, breathe the fresh air, and watch the birds and squirrels at play can be so relaxing and restorative? There is something so powerful, restorative, and energizing about taking time to be in nature—where we can easily see the amazing gift of God's creation and His creative power! He has given us the sea, the stars, the animals, the trees and the flowers as gifts to remind us of how much He loves us and how His power can transform us.

Gain Insight

Answer the questions, be honest with yourself and be transformed!

1. How does being in nature restore your emotional health?

   _____
   _____
   _____

2. When was the last time you paused and noticed God's creation? How did it make you feel?

   _____
   _____
   _____

3. Do you believe God desires to restore you through His creation?

_____
_____
_____

4. Do you believe it blesses God's heart when you thank Him for the beauty He has given to you?

_____
_____
_____

5. When seeing nature, does it help you to see the Lord's provision?

_____
_____
_____

Pray

Father, You are the creator of the world and all the beauty that is in it. Help me to take the time to appreciate the flowers You've created for me, the beautiful skies that testify of You, and everything in nature that You have given to bring me peace. Let the quietness still my heart and bring me closer to You. I love You, Lord, and I am so grateful for Your beautiful creation.

Day 5

Emotional Wellness
Thankful Heart

*"Don't be pulled in different directions or worried about a thing.
Be saturated in prayer throughout each day,
offering your faith-filled requests before God
with overflowing gratitude. Tell him every detail of your life."*
—Philippians 4:6 (TPT)

We live in a world that can surround us with worries, cares, and stresses that can wear us down. Anxiety creates great emotional distress. Fortunately, God has given us a powerful way to combat anxious thoughts and feelings—the gift of gratitude! Thankfulness helps us to bring to the forefront of our mind all the wonderful and good things that God has done for us. It builds up our faith as we are reminded of how trustworthy and loving He is.

Gain Insight

Answer the questions, be honest with yourself and be transformed!

1. Are you experiencing any anxiety or stress currently?

2. How does being thankful shift your perspective?

3. Do you believe God will answer the prayers of your heart?

4. Are you able to trust God?

5. What are some steps you can take to be more thankful and trusting?

Pray

Lord, thank You for Your love and forgiveness toward me. I am so grateful for all that You do for me. Help me to stay focused on all of my blessings and to keep a thankful heart. You are a trustworthy and good God. Give me wisdom on anything causing stress in my life and help me to set boundaries in love. Help me to live in peace with all, so long as it depends on me.

Day 6

Emotional Wellness
Hope

"Now may God, the fountain of hope,
fill you to overflowing with uncontainable joy and perfect peace
as you trust in him. And may the power of the Holy Spirit continually surround
your life with his super-abundance until you radiate with hope!"
—**Romans 15:13 (TPT)**

Just as gratitude can remind us of God's goodness to us, thus bringing balance to our emotions, so too, hope can bring us emotional well-being. The two are tied together—a thankful heart focuses on what God has done for us, while hope points us forward to what we are actively expecting Him to do now and in our future. Placing our hope in Him is powerful because He is trustworthy, and He keeps His promises. When we trust that He has us in His hands, keeping us safe and helping us, we can shift into the healing, energizing place of hope, joy and peace.

Gain Insight

Answer the questions, be honest with yourself and be transformed!

1. What would you like to have hope for?

   _____
   _____
   _____

2. Are you able to have hope while waiting for the answers?

   _____
   _____
   _____

3. What will help you to have the hope that you need?

4. Do you trust God's Word?

5. How does the Holy Spirit empower you to have the hope you need?

Pray

Thank You, Lord Jesus, for filling me with hope! You love me, Lord, and I know You care about what is on my heart. Help me to believe and to stay focused on Your promises. Help me to live a life filled with Your promises and the good future You have prepared for me.

Week Four: Emotional Wellness

Day 7

Emotional Wellness
Sleep

"Now, because of you, Lord,
I will lie down in peace and sleep comes at once,
for no matter what happens, I will live unafraid!"
—**Psalm 4:8 (TPT)**

Sometimes, the simplest things we do to take good care of ourselves can have tremendous impact on our emotional well-being. A great example of this is rest and sleep. You may have noticed how not having enough sleep can make it harder to respond in a godly way to the day's events. A lack of good rest can make us more quick-tempered, or more likely to give in to negative feelings. Good sleep and time for rest and self-care, on the other hand, can help us to be less reactive and more even-keeled, even when unexpected events arise throughout our day.

Gain Insight

Answer the questions, be honest with yourself and be transformed!

1. How does knowing the Lord intimately help you to sleep and rest well?

2. What can you meditate on prior to going to bed?

3. What promises in scripture help you to focus on rest?

   _____
   _____
   _____

4. Does knowing the Lord help you to feel safe? How?

   _____
   _____
   _____

5. Who can you pray for to help them rest well?

   _____
   _____
   _____

Pray

Thank You, Lord, for giving me deep rest no matter what happens. You are my protector, Lord; I trust You with my life. Thank You for giving me a mind that focuses on Your promises. I live to see others come to know You and the sweet sleep that will come to them because of it. You give me peace, Lord, and I am so thankful for You!

Week Four: Emotional Wellness

Reflection for the Week on Emotional Wellness

Answer the questions, be honest with yourself and be transformed!

1. Are you moving closer to your emotional wellness goals?

2. Is there anything getting in the way?

3. Do you need to set any new plans?

4. Have you found an accountability partner?

5. In what ways can you help someone in their emotional life?

Write Your Inner Narration

Using what you have learned from this chapter, the scriptures you have memorized this week, and what you discovered while answering this week's questions, build on your original narration from weeks 1, 2 and 3, and write an additional short godly narration using only positive words. If you find it helpful, review your answers to the daily questions from this week, take note of any positive words, and include them in your new godly narration for this week.

Example: I AM beautiful. I AM loved by God, just as I AM.
I AM forgiven. I AM pleasing to God. I AM strong. I AM courageous.

I AM filled with godly purpose. I AM equipped and able to achieve my godly goals.
I AM a son or a daughter of the King. I AM covered in His grace.
Nothing anyone says or does can harm me because I AM protected.

I AM healthy in my boundaries. I AM forgiving. I AM loved in my relationships.
I AM wise and gracious in my interactions with others in my life.

I AM emotionally well, I AM focused. I AM at peace and rested. I AM balanced. I AM strong.
I AM aware of what I feel and I AM led by God in how to respond to my emotions... etc.

Week Five

Physical Health and Wellness

Our physical health is a very important aspect of our lives—and God desires to see us healthy in body! He also desires to give us the energy we need to be healthy. God is so good. He knows our needs when it comes to our physical condition and our body's wellness. He longs for us to come to Him and to trust Him to fulfill those needs.

There are so many aspects to our physical health that we are going to examine as we seek to transform ourselves in this area of life. So much is going on in our individual lives, and our physical wellness has an impact on all areas of our life. Therefore, it is important to be aware of what is happening in our bodies and to make choices that enhance our health. As we grow in our awareness and improve in our physical wellness, we can apply some of the same principles to improve in the other areas of our life too.

As we begin to look at our physical wellness, let me encourage you that wherever you are at right now, you are loved by God! Though the world often places judgments on physical wellness—harshly criticizing those who look a certain way or are at a certain weight—this is not the way of God. In Him, there is no judgment about how you look. He simply wants us to be well so that we can enjoy the good things He has for us, and so that we can fulfill our God-given purpose in Him.

In addition, I encourage you to be kind to yourself and to others who may be facing physical illness right now. Yes, God wants us well—but He does not judge or condemn us when we are sick. Rather, He has made provision for our healing through Jesus Christ. Health and well-being are areas we can progressively walk in and grow in.

Factors that Affect Physical Wellness

When we consider physical well-being, remember that there are three culprits that can sabotage us—things that we can and should be aware of as we move into our transformation in this area of life.

First, we are living in a broken world. And to some degree, that means there are illnesses, diseases, physical disabilities, and other physical ailments that can arise in our bodies. Parts of our bodies may begin to malfunction—such as an appendix that suddenly becomes inflamed, or a thyroid that begins to underperform or overperform. Often, these situations are the result of the fact that our bodies are subject to the world's brokenness, and they begin to break down over time. In some of these cases of illness and ailments, we may not understand everything that happens—but we can still seek God's healing and embrace the medicines and wellness techniques available to us to improve our health.

Second, we have an enemy, the devil, who looks for opportunities to steal, kill and destroy. There are times that he may attack us with sickness, especially when it interferes with our ability to fulfill something that God has called us to do. Thankfully, in Christ we can take a stand in faith and declare His healing over our bodies. (In fact, there are many scriptures on healing, some of which I'll mention below, that we can use as we pray and believe God for our health.)

And lastly, we are all human and we are fallible. At times, we can fall into patterns and habits of self-sabotage around our physical well-being. This can manifest in so many ways—from eating too much or too little, choosing foods or drinks that are not as healthy or not ideal for our needs (such as eating too much sugar if one is diabetic), failing to exercise regularly, not discussing symptoms with a trusted doctor in a timely fashion, and more. Our choices do have an impact on our physical condition, and so we benefit from being aware of our thinking and making conscious, good decisions for our physical wellness.

The good news is, we can make positive changes and develop good habits so that we can eliminate or take better charge over any tendencies we may have to sabotage ourselves. We can make changes that support our physical health, healing, and wellness.

This decision to be transformed in our habits of physical wellness is so important because we cannot continue to do the same things and expect different results. If we want to see different results in our bodies, we must be willing to change our habits and routines. The great news is that through God's Word and His Holy Spirit, we are empowered to make these changes! As we rely on Him and work on changing our thoughts and habits, we can begin to experience great physical wellness.

Know that God Wants You Well

"Have you forgotten that your body is now
the sacred temple of the Spirit of Holiness, who lives in you?
You don't belong to yourself any longer,
for the gift of God, the Holy Spirit, lives inside your sanctuary."
—**1 Corinthians 6:19 (TPT)**

Being transformed in our bodies begins with our thoughts. As we transform our mindset to focus on a desire to honor God by caring for our body, which is His temple, we will find it easier to make choices that align with how He sees us. We are living sacrifices to Him (Romans 12:1-2), well-loved and treasured, and this includes our physical selves.

Yes, God loves and treasures you just as you are right now. He does not love you any less if your physical health isn't perfect. Remember, though, that there are many benefits to being well that God desires us to enjoy. Good health means it is easier for us to do what we are called to do. Improved physical wellness can improve our mood and give us more energy for the other areas of our life, including our career and our relationships.

So, it is good and useful for us to seek to take the best care of our living temple, our body, as we can. And there are many things we can do to love and treasure our bodies as God does.

For example, many of us desire to arrive at a healthier weight for our height and frame. This is a positive desire, as being a healthy weight can improve how our joints function, how much energy we have throughout the day, our hormonal levels, and more. Therefore, if this is a desire of yours, know that the process of transformation here begins with bringing our eating and exercise habits to the Lord. We are choosing to honor the Lord by caring for our body.

Physically, it's important to realize that it is God's desire for you to be healed and healthy. There are many verses that tell us so! First Peter 2:24 (TPT) tells us, *"He himself carried our sins in his body on the cross so that we would be dead to sin and live for righteousness. Our instant healing flowed from his wounding."*

Jeremiah 30:17 (NIV) says, *"I will restore you to health and heal your wounds, declares the Lord."* Exodus 23:25 (NIV) says, *"Worship the Lord your God, and his blessing will be on your food and water. I will take away sickness from among you."*

Take a look at how these scriptures and others like them point to God as our Healer, and you will begin to develop faith around this truth—He desires to see you healed! The more you believe that He wants you well, the more you will be open to hearing from the Lord and therefore learn how to care for yourself. You will then seek Him to empower you to take the actions necessary to support your wellness.

In addition to what God's Word says regarding the healing of our bodies, God has also given us tools for healthy living, including foods that are beneficial to providing the vitamins and minerals our bodies need for optimal wellness. Most of us know in general what we need to eat for a healthy diet. We all have the ability to dive deeper into learning more about our health, as there are many resources about healthy eating available to us, both online and in bookstores. We also have wellness coaches and classes available to you in our YKI coaching ministry should you decide you want to work with someone to hold you accountable.

An important truth to keep in mind is that we are all unique, and therefore it is important to seek God's help to show us what foods we should eat and what is okay to drink. He will even guide you in how to exercise, and how to further care for your body to experience great health. As we trust that He wants us well and make ourselves available to His guidance, He will lead us to make certain changes that support our physical wellness. He may inspire us to switch up our exercise routine or direct us to cut something out of our diet or add something into our diet that could help us be healthier.

As we are faithful to seek God and make the changes He calls us to make for our physical wellness, we will begin to see the benefits of our obedience and trust. I know this to be true as the Lord healed me from pain and inflammation. I had horrible arthritis in my hands for at least fifteen years. During those years, I continued to seek the Lord and His guidance on what shifts and adjustments I needed to make to be healed. He guided me to the right books to learn more on healthy eating to reduce inflammation. I implemented these new habits and continued to keep the faith that God would heal me—and He did! It has now been three years since I have experienced arthritis.

So often, our physical health has connections to what is happening in our emotions and our spiritual condition. Remember, all the areas of the circle connect! When I began to look for solutions for the inflammation I was facing, I sought the Lord in body, mind, and spirit. I wanted to know if there was a spiritual connection associated with my physical pain—and I believe there was. Arthritis has to do with control, and there were areas of control that I sought to have concerning a difficult relationship in my life. Once I learned to surrender that relationship to the Lord, letting Him take control, while choosing to walk in obedience to Him body, mind, and spirit, I found complete healing—complete wellness in body, mind, and spirit.

When we follow His guidance on how to care for our body, we will feel better. He will guide us into the ways that create greater physical well-being. All glory to the Lord for being such a good Father and for His great wisdom and direction to help us create health in our bodies!

The Spiritual Connection to Physical Wellness

"Beloved friend, I pray that you are prospering in every way and that you continually enjoy good health, just as your soul is prospering."
—3 John 1:2 (TPT)

Good physical health begins with our mind and spirit. If we are wounded mentally or spiritually, we need to get that area of our life healed so that our physical bodies will be well. We see this in the Scriptures. As we read the Gospels, we often see that there is a spiritual component to healing. Therefore, this area of our life is a good place to start if we are seeking God's wisdom about how we can improve our health.

Often, Jesus would meet someone who was facing a physical illness, and His first step was to forgive them of their sin (Matthew 9:1-8, Psalm 103:3, John 5:14). And then, after forgiveness, healing could come in and make them whole. Healing often begins in our spirit and soul first, then in our bodies.

So, when we are dealing with a physical issue—such as the pain and inflammation I mentioned earlier—it is a wise approach to also ask the Lord if there are any spiritual issues we must address. Ask Him to search you and let you know if there is anything that needs to be dealt with. There may be fears and frustrations to ask forgiveness for. Perhaps you may simply need to put your focus back on the Lord.

At times, the Lord may even lead you to a short period of fasting that can help you to reset yourself spiritually and physically. The act of fasting in a healthy way has health benefits as well as spiritual benefits. It can help us to practice self-control over body, mind, and spirit. Jesus has self-control, and we are to be like Him, even with our bodies.

If you choose to fast, I encourage you to look for good, reliable information on ways to safely do so. You may even wish to consult a nutritionist or a doctor for guidance in this area. And remember, food is not the only type of fasting you can do. The Lord may lead you to fast from a certain food, or even something you are watching or doing. If He leads you to fast, use that opportunity to spend more time with Him in prayer, allowing Him to guide you into the knowledge you need for better physical wellness.

As we honor God with our bodies, He will reward us with health and many other blessings like peace, contentment, and satisfaction. Do whatever He instructs you to do concerning your physical wellness and make the decision to act according to His guidance. His plans for you are good, and they are intended to bless you. You will benefit when you follow through.

Managing Stress Helps Our Physical Wellness

The Lord tells us so many times in the Bible not to fear—because He knows how fear creates stress that can hurt our bodies, increasing hormones like cortisol and adrenaline within us that can, over time and continued exposure, wear down our immune system. Yet we live in a world that often provokes a lot of stress in our lives. We're bombarded with negative news. We're taught to worry about our safety and our finances and our home life. It is no wonder that so many people face stress-related illnesses.

In addition, we're encouraged to be on the go all the time. This constant, hectic, stress-centered lifestyle can be hard on our bodies. But there are a number of ways we can reduce our stress, lessen anxiety, and support our physical wellness. God will give us guidance as to how to do so in ways that sustain us, strengthen us, and bring us peace. The key is awareness—and we can ask the Lord to show us what our bodies need.

One example is breathing. Did you know that deep breathing is super healthy for our bodies? Our physical bodies tend toward acidity, but deep breaths bring us into better balance, producing an alkalizing effect that is good for us. Deep breathing helps us to be calm by engaging the parasympathetic nervous system, which relaxes our physical body. Deep breaths can lower our stress, clear our lungs, relieve our pain, and get rid of toxins in the body.

Yet it's easy to find ourselves engaging in shallow breathing without even realizing it. As you pay attention to your body and your breathing, you may find the Lord prompting you to breathe more deeply. He may also encourage you to take time for other activities that are calming stress relievers for you—such as getting a massage, attending exercise classes, going for a walk outdoors, having a relaxing cup of tea, or taking a warm bath. Making time to ease stress is good not only for your mind and emotions, but also for your physical body.

As we gain awareness of how we are feeling—physically and emotionally—we become better equipped to make simple choices such as taking time for stress-relieving activities. And this supports our physical wellness.

Creating Healthy Eating Habits that Fit You

God has given us so many good foods that are nourishing for our bodies. He has provided fruits, vegetables, grains, and meat for us to sustain ourselves. As we learn more about healthy eating, we'll see the benefits in our physical bodies.

Our world often encourages us to eat and drink things that are not good for us, and that act as toxins. Examples are too much sugar and alcohol, which can make our physical bodies sick. Ailments such as inflammation, weight gain, headaches, aches and pain, and chronic fatigue can arise when we choose to eat and drink substances that are not healthy for our body.

And since we are all unique, some of what is considered healthy for one person may not be a fit for all of us. For example, you may have a food allergy to a certain food that is generally considered good for the body. Or your body may have a harder time digesting certain foods that others can easily enjoy. Perhaps it is not good for you personally to eat kale even though others may eat it and have no problems. As you allow the Lord to speak to you and listen closely to His guidance, He will give you specific direction that is for your best interest.

There are so many food choices today. Fortunately, God will guide us in developing healthy eating habits that work for us as unique individuals. We can learn to be aware of what foods support our physical well-being and choose to make them a part of our regular diet. If you would like to make changes in this area, a good place to begin is to consider how God made you, and what He has designed you to eat. There are many great books and online resources to help with this.

Sadly, the world tends to focus on food choices and diet as something to address only when people want to lose weight. And the world tends to emphasize the negative aspects of it, telling us it's hard, and it's no fun, but that we must torture ourselves to be a weight that others find attractive.

Yet dieting isn't just about weight loss. It is a valuable means of supporting our bodies and caring for our wellness throughout our lives. And diet can change depending on the time of life you're in, specific needs you have, what's available seasonally in your area, and so much more. This is where becoming educated about healthy food and drink habits can really do us so much good.

For example, there are times when you or someone you care about needs to incorporate different foods for current physical needs. Perhaps you need more complex carbohydrates to get more energy, or more protein to build more muscle because you are training to run a marathon. Or perhaps you realize you need to lessen your caffeine intake and drink more water instead to enjoy calmer mornings. There are so many reasons to shift our diets, even on a day-to-day basis.

Developing a healthy mindset around food choices is essential to sticking to a good diet that supports our health. I encourage you *not* to think in terms of all or nothing. That mindset can paralyze you and make it harder to make good choices around food and physical health. An all-or-nothing mentality is not sustainable.

Instead, find ways to allow an ebb and flow in your life, so that you can make healthy eating habits easier to maintain long-term. As you listen to God's direction concerning what you eat, you will recognize when it's ok to treat yourself to something you don't normally eat—such as at a family gathering when it's appropriate to have a piece of cake. And you'll also be able to make good decisions to say no to something when it's appropriate—such as saying no to coffee when you know it will make you more stressed if you drink it.

It helps to be mindful that food is a gift from the Lord. And it is something we can choose and have control over, rather than something that controls us. As the saying goes, we eat to live—we don't live to eat.

The Power of Exercise

One of the most important ways that we can care for our physical well-being is to make time in our routine for regular exercise. Physical movement is so healthy for our muscles, our joints, our digestion, and our circulation. Developing an exercise routine is something we should aim to make a part of our long-term lifestyle. It requires planning, though, because so much of the modern lifestyle keeps us sedentary. It's all too easy not to move as much as we need to.

Like all things that transform us, the key to managing an exercise routine is discovering the right fit for your personal needs, preferences, and circumstances. What works for someone else may not be the right fit for you. I know some people who run marathons regularly, and I know others who take walks and do yoga. There are many positive ways to get the exercise we need.

One good place to get started is to consult with your doctor to see what he or she recommends for you, given any health issues you are dealing with. From there, you can get guidance from a personal trainer, or do some research on ways to ease into a new exercise routine. You might begin with walks in the park or around your neighborhood, and slowly build up to the exercises you would like to do more of.

Another key to building a successful exercise routine is realizing that it will ebb and flow. Just like your eating habits may need to be adjusted temporarily to different situations and seasons, so may your exercise routines need to shift and change. Perhaps an injury or surgery requires you to slow down for a while. Or perhaps a weight loss goal requires you to work out a little longer each day. Sometimes, you may need to fit in a quick walk around the block because your schedule that day is so full.

All these choices can be good, as long as you are maintaining your awareness of what your body needs, what you can fit into your schedule, and what God is leading you to do. Making healthy choices for our bodies means finding what fits your unique body, and God will guide you in that.

Balancing Appearance and Well-Being

I realize that by addressing eating habits and exercise and physical wellness, many people immediately think of issues such as weight and appearance. Therefore, I'd like to take time to discuss this issue, as it can very much be part of our physical well-being.

I would never want anyone to feel judged about their appearance. How we look is an outward thing, and the Bible tells us clearly that God looks at our heart (1 Samuel 16:7). He is concerned about what is happening within us, our motives, our pureness, our love for Him and for others. A beautiful outward appearance cannot substitute for a godly, loving heart that pleases the Lord.

Yet the Bible also tells us to create a rapport with others, to respect ourselves and others, and to be an example to bring glory to the Lord. We are to honor the Lord with our body. Our appearance can be a part of this process of caring for ourselves and interacting with others to lead them to the Lord. People are drawn to those who look good, who dress well, who are healthy, and who are taking good care of themselves.

Imagine, for example, that you are moving in the right direction with your body. Perhaps you are toned up and looking healthier. People around you will notice the changes and be interested in what you've done and how you've achieved it. Or perhaps you have received a healing from making proper choices. The glory of these rewards belongs to Jesus. Share with others how God led you to great health. These blessings are part of your testimony and should be shared with others to help lead them to the Lord and thus glorify Him. This is very exciting!

First Corinthians 10:31 (TPT) says, *"Whether you eat or drink, live your life in a way that glorifies and honors God."* Whatever we do should honor Him and bring Him glory, and that includes how we appear and how we dress. Therefore, as you consider your physical appearance, ask the Lord what would honor

Him best. Ask Him if your appearance is helping you to win other people to Christ, or if there are things He would have you change so that you can draw others to Him more effectively.

Living with Confidence

Our physical health and appearance should reflect the joy in our hearts and our confidence in who we are in Christ. It's not based solely on outer things, but also, it's about who we are on the inside. Confidence is not only about how we look. It's about trusting God and respecting ourselves.

As we walk closely with the Lord and become more confident in who He has created us to be, that assurance and peace gets reflected on the outside. And we can find it easier to maintain good healthy habits as a result of this deep self-assurance that comes from knowing and loving the Lord. He gives us the power to overcome that which isn't good for us!

Building confidence in the area of our health comes as we apply the 5 Keys to Success in this sphere of our life. As we recognize what is true, set goals, make plans, and take action to follow through, we start to experience successful transformations in our physical bodies. We start to see the positive results of making healthy choices about what we eat and drink, how we exercise, and how we dress.

When we do what we say we are going to do, we feel better about ourselves—which helps us to continue to make good choices in every area of life, including our health and fitness. Imagine following up on your commitment to lose weight, or eat more vegetables, or exercise more regularly. As you accomplish these goals with the Lord's help, you will grow more confident in who you are in Him. You'll experience the joy that comes with caring for yourself with Godly wisdom.

Self-Care and Self-Control

There was such a swirl of activity around Jesus, with so many people coming and going, that they were unable to even eat a meal. So Jesus said to his disciples, 'Come, let's take a break and find a secluded place where you can rest a while.'"
—Mark 6:31 (TPT)

So much of our success in the area of our physical well-being comes down to developing a mindset of caring for ourselves with a sense of discipline, planning and choice. Jesus modeled wise self-care and disciplined decision-making so beautifully in the Scriptures for us. As we read the Gospels, we can see that He regularly took time to rest when He needed it. He ate when He needed to, and He fed others when they were hungry. He fasted when God led Him to do so, and He ate with friends too.

Jesus tended to His physical well-being, so that He could continue to minister to others effectively. And we can and should follow His example in this area. Remember, God has called us to care about our well-being. We are called to have self-control as well. *"For God will never give you the spirit of fear, but the Holy Spirit who gives you mighty power, love, and self-control"* (2 Timothy 1:7 TPT). As we engage in responsible self-care, we can grow in physical wellness, which glorifies God.

As you give attention to this area of life, keep in mind that the tools we've already discussed in this book can help you achieve success. Use the 5 Keys to Success to assess where you are now in your physical wellness, decide where you would like to be and set the goals and their purpose. Set a plan that will help you move towards improved health.

Become aware of how you currently think about your body, food, drink, exercise, and appearance. What are your thoughts about these areas? Are they filled with shame? Have you been told negative things about your body? Do you tend to feel that you don't have what it takes to be your ideal weight? Perhaps you are not confident about how you look, or you worry that others will not find you attractive. Or perhaps you have dealt with an illness and have come to think that you will never feel better.

As we identify these thoughts, we can begin to address them with what the Bible says is true about us. God's Word tells us that we are healed, that we have been made whole, that we can be forgiven, that we are fearfully and wonderfully made. Rejecting any lies we have been told about our physical bodies and embracing God's healing power is essential to our self-care and our blossoming into better well-being.

There are so many ways in which your mindset can be transformed so that you can enjoy greater freedom as well as greater physical wellness. Awareness is key to showing you the ways in which you can move forward into what the Lord has for you. Once you know where you are at right now, you can choose the destination you want to aim for.

Set goals to reach that destination and also become aware of the purpose behind your goal, because your purpose will drive you to reach your goal. For example, it's not enough to just desire to lose weight; you must also find the purpose for that weight loss. Perhaps your purpose is to set an example to your family on how you care for your temple, thus drawing them closer to the Lord. Your purpose will then give greater meaning to your goal and provide great motivation to help you to achieve it.

Use godly I AM statements and the anchoring technique to declare over yourself what God says is true about you in the area of physical wellness. You're a beautiful, living sacrifice to the Lord, a well-loved child of God who is empowered by the Holy Spirit to walk in wellness. You are healed by His stripes and made whole in every area of life. You are a beautiful example to your family on caring for one's temple. Empower yourself with words like, "I AM in control of my intake of food; I decide when I AM full. I can do all things through Christ who gives me strength."

I encourage you to anchor yourself in your identity in Christ at least twice a day, especially as you build new habits around your physical health and well-being. Also, write an inner narration that you can read daily and use in your prayer time as you move daily toward greater physical wellness.

As you follow the 4th Key to Success, which is taking the action steps toward the physical wellness you desire, it's a good idea to have an accountability partner to help you follow through. You will then reap the 5th Key of Success, the reward of achieving your physical wellness goals as you continue to lean on the Lord to help you. You will be a pillar example of good health, one who is able to share with others how God transformed your health. What an exciting and wonderful blessing that will be!

Day 1

Physical Health
Living Sacrifice

*"Beloved friends, what should be our proper response to God's marvelous mercies?
To surrender yourselves to God to be his sacred, living sacrifices.
And live in holiness, experiencing all that delights his heart.
For this becomes your genuine expression of worship."*
—**Romans 12:1 (TPT)**

Do you realize that your physical body is as much of a vehicle you can use to honor the Lord as your prayers, your giving, and your sharing of the Gospel? Yes, it's true! God desires us to take good care of our bodies as an act of worship to Him. After all, being physically healthy often makes it easier to do the things we are called to do in the Lord—including our career, our ministry, our parenting, and so much more.

Gain Insight

Answer the questions, be honest with yourself and be transformed!

1. How does offering yourself as a sacrifice bring you closer to God?

2. Since you are a living sacrifice, should you be pure and holy as an offering?

Week Five: Physical Health and Wellness

3. How can you tend to yourself to make sure you are a pleasing sacrifice?

4. How do you think Jesus took care of His physical health?

5. How does your physical health affect your spirit and mind?

Pray

Lord Jesus, help me to live in a way that is pleasing to You. Help me to care for my physical health, making good choices about my eating habits, exercise, and physical self-care, which shows I value the life You have given to me. Help me to be pure and holy as a living sacrifice to You.

Day 2

Physical Health
Healthy Choices

"And God said: '
I give you every seed-bearing plant growing throughout
the earth, vegetables, and every fruit-bearing tree with its seed
within itself. They will be your food.'"
—Genesis 1:29 (TPT)

When you bring God into your healthy eating, it changes everything. Striving to honor Him in your food and drink choices will bring not only a heart change, but it will also change your choices. And this will help you to use His wisdom in order to walk in the health He desires you to enjoy.

Gain Insight

Answer the questions, be honest with yourself and be transformed!

1. Are fruits and vegetables something you include in your daily food choices?

2. Are you living sober, free from drugs and alcohol?

3. Do you take the time to thank the Lord for the food He has given to you?

4. How balanced are your eating habits?

5. Do you take the time to learn more about nutrition?

Pray

Thank You, Lord, for the healthy foods that You have created for me to eat. Help me to be mindful of my food choices so I can live a healthy and balanced life. Help me to prepare healthy foods and to learn more about the proper nutrition my body needs.

Day 3

Physical Health
Exercise

*"But I train like a champion athlete.
I subdue my body and get it under my control, so that after preaching
the good news to others I myself won't be disqualified."*
—**1 Corinthians 9:27 (ESV)**

Taking care of our physical well-being involves a certain amount of discipline and dedication to doing what is good for our body—and this includes exercise. Moving and staying active is so good for us! And there are so many ways we can stay active and exercise to stay fit. As we do, the positive results will spill over into the other areas of our life too!

Gain Insight

Answer the questions, be honest with yourself and be transformed!

1. What are your current exercise habits?

2. How does exercising your body help you to feel disciplined and in control?

3. What new exercise class or routine would you like to begin?

4. Are you thankful that your body is able to exercise?

5. What healthy foods can you eat prior to exercise? After exercise?

Pray

Thank You, Lord, for a healthy body that is able to exercise. Help me to make it a daily habit to do something to keep myself physically fit. Help me to keep a good attitude about exercise and to be an example to others of how to care for our physical health.

Day 4

Physical Health
Balance

*"It's true that our freedom allows us to do anything,
but that doesn't mean that everything we do is good for us.
I'm free to do as I choose, but I choose to never be enslaved to anything."*
—**1 Corinthians 6:12 (TPT)**

God does not desire us to be obsessed about outward appearances. Rather, He encourages us as His children to walk in a balanced way so that every area of our life is doing well. As we think about how to enhance our physical wellness, we can keep this scripture from 1 Corinthians in mind, asking ourselves, "Is eating this, drinking this, or doing this particular exercise serving me well and supporting my emotional wellness, my relational wellness, and the other areas of my life?" If it is, that's great! If it's not, then let the Lord show you how to make adjustments so that you can pursue physical health in a balanced way.

Gain Insight

Answer the questions, be honest with yourself and be transformed!

1. How does having balance help you to go the distance?

2. What are some things you can do to help you live a more balanced life?

Week Five: Physical Health and Wellness

3. Are you aware and mindful of when your balance has diminished?

4. How does knowing the Lord keep you balanced?

5. Does having a schedule help you to keep a balanced life?

Pray

Thank You, Lord, that You care for me and know what is best for me. Help me to seek Your direction for my life each day as I make decisions about what to do. Keep me balanced so I can go the distance in all things.

Day 5

Physical Health
Purity

> *"Have you forgotten that your body is now the sacred temple of the Spirit of Holiness, who lives in you? You don't belong to yourself any longer, for the gift of God, the Holy Spirit, lives inside your sanctuary. You were God's expensive purchase, paid for with tears of blood, so by all means, then, use your body to bring glory to God!"*
> —1 Corinthians 6:19–20 (TPT)

Caring for our physical well-being involves every way in which we use our body. Staying pure means avoiding things that can lead us into sin and create imbalances in every area of life. We glorify the Lord when we choose what is good and godly, consistent with His Word and His will for our life and saying no to things that can be harmful to us.

Gain Insight

Answer the questions, be honest with yourself and be transformed!

1. What does God have to say about living a pure life?

2. What are the benefits of honoring God by being sexually pure?

Week Five: Physical Health and Wellness

3. How does keeping yourself pure from harmful substances like drugs and alcohol benefit you?

4. How does seeking the Holy Spirit empower you to have self-control?

5. What is your favorite scripture on purity?

Pray

Lord, thank You for Your forgiveness toward me. I am so grateful for all that You do for me. Help me to forgive others their trespasses. Help me to use wisdom when reconciling with others. Help me to live at peace with all people so long as it depends on me. Help me to set boundaries in love.

Day 6

Physical Health
Energy

*"A joyful, cheerful heart brings healing to both body and soul.
But the one whose heart is crushed struggles with sickness and depression."*
—**Proverbs 17:22 (TPT)**

The mind and the body are so intimately connected! When our emotional life is balanced and healthy, it contributes greatly to our physical well-being too. The Word of God reminds us that being joyful in the Lord, trusting and hoping in Him, and resting confidently on His promises promote our health, while negative thinking, discouragement, and anxiety can wear us down physically. So it's important to be aware of how our attitudes, thoughts, and emotions may be affecting our physical energy and well-being.

Gain Insight

Answer the questions, be honest with yourself and be transformed!

1. How does keeping your mind and attitude healthy affect your energy?

2. What are you currently doing to increase your energy?

3. Are there people in your life that drain your energy?

4. Who in your life gives you more energy and strength?

5. Are you getting enough sleep for your day ahead?

Pray

Lord, help me to be wise and discerning about what and who I allow into my life. Help me to fill my life with healthy people who encourage me and give me more energy. Help me to be aware of my sleep and other needs that will give me energy for my days.

Day 7

Physical Health
Rest

"Now I can say to myself and to all, 'Relax and rest, be confident and serene, for the Lord rewards fully those who simply trust in him.'"
—**Psalm 116:7 (TPT)**

Our bodies very much need rest so we can physically recuperate, be strengthened, and reenergized to live our daily lives for the Lord. Restoration—taking time to rest—is as needful as exercising, eating well, and making good choices. Rest is important not just in times we are feeling "under the weather," but also when we are doing well. Remember—it's all about balance! Look for ways to balance your physical activities with times of relaxing restoration.

Gain Insight

Answer the questions, be honest with yourself and be transformed!

1. What type of rest do you take to allow your body to heal?

2. Are you mindful of when your body needs rest from exercise and other things?

3. Do you sleep well at night?

4. What can you do to improve your sleep?

5. Are you eating or drinking anything that interferes with your sleep?

Pray

Lord, help me to be aware of anything that gets in the way of my rest and sleep. Help me to live at peace with all, so that relationships do not disturb my rest. Help me to trust You and to lean on You for my peace. Give me deep sleep and plenty of rest for my days ahead.

Reflection for the Week on Physical Health

Answer the questions, be honest with yourself and be transformed!

1. Are you moving closer to your physical health goals?

2. Is there anything getting in the way?

3. Do you need to set any new plans?

4. Have you found an accountability partner?

5. In what ways can you help someone in their physical health?

Week Five: Physical Health and Wellness

Write Your Inner Narration

Using what you have learned from this chapter, the scriptures you have memorized this week, and what you discovered while answering this week's questions, build on your original narration from weeks 1, 2, 3 and 4, and write an additional short godly narration using only positive words. If you find it helpful, review your answers to the daily questions from this week, take note of any positive words, and include them in your new godly narration for this week.

*Example: I AM beautiful. I AM loved by God, just as I AM.
I AM forgiven. I AM pleasing to God. I AM strong. I AM courageous.*

*I AM filled with godly purpose. I AM equipped and able to achieve my godly goals.
I AM a son or a daughter of the King. I AM covered in His grace.
Nothing anyone says or does can harm me because I AM protected.*

*I AM healthy in my boundaries. I AM forgiving. I AM loved in my relationships.
I AM wise and gracious in my interactions with others in my life.*

*I AM emotionally well, I AM focused. I AM at peace and rested. I AM balanced.
I AM aware of what I feel and I AM led by God in how to respond to my emotions.*

*I AM strong in my body. I AM led by God in what to eat and drink for my health and well-being.
I make time for exercise and rest because I AM caring for my body, which is the temple of the Holy Spirit... etc.*

_____

_____

_____

_____

_____

_____

_____

Week Six

Career and Ministry

In our work-focused, accomplishment-driven world, what we do for a career can seem to define who we are to those around us. You may have noticed that when meeting someone for the first time, people often ask, "What do you do for a living?" In fact, we're so accustomed to defining ourselves by our work that when we're asked to tell someone about ourselves, we often default right to discussing our job or role in our household. Yet our career in life is so much more than that. God has a bigger plan for us than that! You may not have thought about it this way before, but everything we do in life is a form of ministry. Now, ministry means more than having a formal role in the church, such as being a pastor. Whether we are a full-time worker at the church, a volunteer, a businessperson in the marketplace, or holding down an important role in our home (such as a stay-at-home mom), we all have a ministry that God has given us.

Ministry is simply any way in which we serve others, which can include being a loving parent to your children, a godly coworker at the office, a coach for Christ with YKI coaching, and so much more. So, as we talk about career, keep this concept in mind. Your job, or any work you do, is a ministry.

Offering Our Gifts to Others

"God surveyed all he had made and said, 'I love it!'
For it pleased him greatly.
Evening gave way to morning—day six."
—Genesis 1:31 (TPT)

Just as God the Father labored with passion and purpose to do the good work of creating the world, we also are to work and bring benefits to the world around us. Our work can be so much more than just a way to earn an income to pay our bills and provide for our basic needs. The work we do, whether in our career or in service to others, is something that we can enjoy, that we can do with purpose, and that we can be satisfied with—even as we are also making a difference that benefits those around us.

You will notice that I have combined career and ministry in this chapter, and that is purposeful. The world tends to limit career to those who earn an income, and at times even more narrowly, to those who hold specific positions of worldly power and prestige such as CEOs, attorneys, and doctors. In this way, the world often assigns importance based on the career we have—but God doesn't.

God takes a much greater view of this area of our life. He does not think more highly of us when we hold a powerful position or are a celebrity. He does not think lowly of us when we hold jobs that are not at the top of the ladder. In His eyes, everyone has a valuable role to play in supporting others and representing His kingdom. Whether you're a CEO or a janitor, or anything else you can imagine, He loves you and values any good work that you do.

God has created us to be creative like He is, and He has placed dreams in our hearts to achieve. The work we do in this world is to be a tool that aids us in accomplishing our dreams and creating good things that bless us and others. This means it's important to be aware of where He would have us spend our time working and serving others.

Now, this doesn't mean that everyone is to make an income. There are several areas of influence in which we can work and be productive, and some are not tied to making a salary. These roles are just as vital to the Lord as paying positions. But regardless of where you are working and putting forth effort to achieve godly goals, you are meant to be successful. That is God's best and highest for you.

Work and Purpose Go Hand in Hand

God has a purpose and a plan for every single individual on this planet. It doesn't matter who you are, where you've come from, the mistakes that you've made, or anything in your past. It doesn't matter how others define you or the labels they try to place on you. It doesn't matter if you are "somebody" in the way the world defines it, or whether you hold an "important" position in the eyes of the world or not. Every one of us has great value to the Lord, and He desires to put us in the right places where we can be a blessing. (I call these areas mountains of influence, which I'll talk about in more depth below.)

You may have a clear sense of your God-given purpose right now in your career, your ministry, and any work you do at home and in volunteer spaces. If so, this chapter will ground you in that sense of mission and strengthen you in it.

Or perhaps you are wondering where you fit in, unsure of what God desires for you to accomplish. Perhaps you are frustrated with your job or other roles right now, and don't know what to do next. This chapter is for you as well. It will help you to expand your view so that you can see the wondrous possibilities God has for you in terms of the work you do, the ministry you offer to those around you, and the other roles you may hold in your life right now.

Never forget—God has a purpose for you. He has put desires in your heart so you can achieve them, and this includes dreams of holding a specific job, excelling in a chosen career, being a parent, or serving others in various positions of ministry and charity work. These godly dreams and desires are there to fulfill His purpose for our life; they are not an accident. God places them within us and then empowers us to accomplish them. In this way, as we carry out what He has put in our heart to do, we can be an influence on the world for good and thus fulfill the great commission to bring others into God's kingdom.

When we pursue godly desires that line up with His Word, He provides a way for us to be able to excel in those things. Our dreams and desires have a place and are very important to the Lord. This is one reason it is so key to spend time listening to His direction for our life and line ourselves up with His will.

> *"We have become his poetry, a re-created people that will fulfill the destiny*
> *he has given each of us, for we are joined to Jesus, the Anointed One.*
> *Even before we were born, God planned in advance our destiny*
> *and the good works we would do to fulfill it!"*
> **—Ephesians 2:10 (TPT)**

God has prepared good work for us to do. He desires for us to work and be productive and creative in every role we have in our life. In fact, He has placed that desire for productivity within us, a drive to achieve and to be successful in life. Career and ministry tie into this desire for godly accomplishment to further His kingdom, which blesses us and others.

Don't let fear of the unknown paralyze you. Whatever is in your heart to accomplish, get out there and do it! God wants you to have adventures and live fully. If your dream lines up with His Word, the Bible and is a godly goal, you can be sure He has called you to do it—so step out in faith.

God will bless you as you draw near to Him for strength, insight, and encouragement to pursue and achieve your dreams. He will give you great success as you seek to help others and influence them in godly ways.

Knowing What We Are Called to Do

> *"I will instruct you and teach you in the way you should go;*
> *I will counsel you with my loving eye on you."*
> **—Psalm 32:8 (NIV)**

A common refrain I hear in my coaching sessions with others is that they do not know what they should do for a career. Sometimes, they feel they are in the wrong job and genuinely are confused about what would fit them better as a career. Other times, people tell me they have dreams for a certain career on their hearts, but they do not know how to begin moving toward achieving that dream. And sometimes, they feel guilty about pursuing the work they feel led most to do, because of what others say or because of limiting beliefs they have been taught.

God's plan for your life includes any work, ministry and serving you do. God will impress upon your heart what to do and you will know it—remember our YKI mantra—You Know It! That knowledge of what He has called you to do is within you. As you spend time with Him in prayer and meditating on His Word, He will begin to instruct you and tell you what way to go, just as Psalm 32:8 promises. He has counsel to offer concerning this area of your life!

In addition to spending time with the Lord, there are some practical steps you can take to identify jobs and ministry spaces where you will do well. Use the 5 Keys to Success and ask yourself what is true about yourself.

What are your talents and strengths? Do you have any specific skills that you particularly excel at? What do other people say you are good at? Do any of those talents open an avenue where you can either earn an income or be of service to others as a blessing unto the Lord?

If you are not sure of your strengths or feel that you need more direction in this area, there are so many assessment tools you can use. Many of these tools are online, and they are free to use. And you can also reach out to one of our coaches for help in pinpointing what you are good at and what careers align with your unique skills.

What dreams do you have in your heart? Are there any careers or acts of service that particularly appeal to you? What would you need to do to enter those areas of work or ministry? Do they require a certification you must earn? A degree or specific form of education?

Remember that today, between online training opportunities and in-person classes, there are many routes to gain any education and certification you need to move forward in a chosen career. If you are concerned about the costs, remember that there may even be opportunities to finance tuition through your current job, scholarships, and grants. God is a great Provider, and as you take steps of faith on the path He has set before you, you can trust Him and expect Him to provide what you need to be successful.

Take time to make connections as well, so that others around you know what you desire to do in terms of career, ministry, and volunteering. God loves to work through us to bless others—and He loves to work through others to bless us! So, it is no surprise that He can and will use our relationships and our network to help us move forward in our godly calling. If you know someone who holds the career you desire to have, learn from them. Ask them how they came into their role, and what was most helpful for them in getting there.

And finally, know that it is okay, even good, to put yourself out into the marketplace. If you have a business, don't be afraid to market it. God is not against us promoting the work we do, so long as we are doing it as unto Him and representing Him well through honest, quality work. If you have accomplished something valuable in the workplace and with others, proudly display that on your resume. These accomplishments can help you move into your next role.

When you step into your new position or excel in your career, remember that it is the Lord who has blessed you and caused you to prosper. Give praise to Him and honor Him by also blessing others. In this way, He will continue to work through you, and you will continue to receive His blessings!

The Seven Mountains of Influence

"God, keep us near your mercy-fountain and bless us! And when you
look down on us, may your face beam with joy! Send us out
all over the world so that everyone everywhere will discover your ways
and know who you are and see your power to save."
—Psalm 67:1–2 (NIV)

As we talk about finding places to serve in our career or ministry, I encourage you to think about all the places in your life in which you serve others. We all hold more than one role in life. For example, you may be a mother and a wife and a teacher in your local school system. Or you may be a son, a banker, and an usher in your church. These areas of service can be called "mountains of influence"—places where we can make a difference in the lives of others.

There are seven mountains of influence where you may have a role to play—areas including government, media, arts and entertainment, business, education, religion, and family. As you meditate and pray about God's purpose for your life, He may reveal that He has plans for you to pay a role in many of these mountains of influence. As we discuss career and ministry in this chapter and in the activities that follow, you may wish to apply what you learn to any of these mountains of influence—so that you can be a greater blessing anywhere you serve others.

> *"Put your heart and soul into every activity you do,*
> *as though you are doing it for the Lord himself and not merely for others.*
> *For we know that we will receive a reward, an inheritance from the*
> *Lord, as we serve the Lord Yahweh, the Anointed One!"*
> **—Colossians 3:23–24 (TPT)**

As this verse of scripture makes clear, we have a great influence on the world—in every role we hold. And since we spend so much of our daily life at our place of business, as well as caring for family and doing other work, it makes sense that our career and ministry area of life is something we should pay close attention to. As we are working and serving others, we have so many opportunities throughout our day to speak into the lives of those around us.

We are serving the Lord when we glorify Him in our career and ministry, in our families, and in all the areas where we serve others! Through these many roles we take on over the course of our lives, there is an opportunity to influence others in a way that shines light on that which is good. This will increase our chance to bring them into a relationship with Jesus. We can bring His kingdom here on earth through our areas of influence, including your career as well as other areas of service. For this reason, we are called to work as unto the Lord.

We are to be the hands, feet, and mouthpiece of the Lord. This makes our beliefs about God, ourselves, our abilities, and what we do in this world so very important. Our beliefs will shine through our works to those in our sphere of influence. What we believe about our career and ministry becomes key to our success and how we give back.

God has created you to be resourceful, creative, and productive. No matter your age, you still have something to contribute and something to say. You will have a sphere of influence until you are no longer here on this earth. So, as you consider career and ministry, keep in mind that you have many places where you can set your hands to work for the good of God's Kingdom. These mountains of influence can involve both the professional things you do as well as and any other form of work and service that does not provide a salary.

Government: The First Mountain of Influence

The first area of influence to discuss is that of government. We have all been designed to govern in some fashion. Our world needs godly government to meet the needs of the people and to keep peace in our nation and world. As we look at our world today and see the needs, and the questions, and the conflicts that arise in our nation, it is clear that we would benefit from having people who are godly in government positions.

We need people who are called to serve in this area to rise up and take their place. You may or may not hold this as a full-time career, or you may serve voluntarily or part-time, such as serving at polling places or registering voters or holding a position on a local municipal council.

Even if you are not called to serve formally in government, something we can all do is pray for the governing bodies and elected officials and their staff. We can pray for more godly leaders to step up and fill the positions God desires them to have.

> *"Most of all, I'm writing to encourage you to pray with gratitude to God.*
> *Pray for all men with all forms of prayers and requests as you intercede*
> *with intense passion. And pray for every political leader and representative,*
> *so that we would be able to live tranquil, undisturbed lives,*
> *as we worship the awe-inspiring God with pure hearts."*
> **—1 Timothy 2:1–2 (TPT)**

God's Word instructs us to pray for all who are in authority, and as we take that godly position to pray for those who govern us, we are helping to have an influence on this first mountain. We can pray that their hearts will be open, and that God will lead them in the right direction as they make decisions that have an effect on how we live.

Most importantly, we are all to exercise the rights we have been given to vote. We must educate ourselves and vote for those who are godly and who represent godly values. This will help our government move in the right direction, helping our nation to prosper. We can also participate in open governmental forums and public meetings where there are opportunities for our voice to be heard as issues are decided.

Media: The Second Mountain of Influence

The media has great influence on our culture. And so, it is important that godly voices be heard through every media channel that exists—television, movies, websites, magazines, social media, radio and more. Whether it is through a full-time paid career in a media position, or whether it is through a social media channel where we share positive, uplifting thoughts, beautiful things that God has made, and inspirational words of faith, we can have an influence in this arena of life.

As godly messages and encouragement are shared through different media, people in the audience can be drawn to the Lord. Therefore, as we share posts on our social media and participate in this area, we should be glorifying God. We want to portray light and goodness so that when others see what we are sharing, they are drawn to what is good and godly.

Therefore, we must consider what we are putting out into the world. Are our social media posts positive and God-focused? Are our photos appropriate and modest? Are we sharing videos and memes that are kind, rather than mean-spirited or judgmental?

And for those who hold careers in the media, such as journalists, it is so important for them to be truth-bearers. We need people who will step up in this field to share godly truth. As with government, we can pray for people in the media to do what is good and reflect what is godly to the world. If we see things that are not godly, we can notify those who are in positions that can seek to change it. We must make our voices heard and challenge those in position to keep good content.

Arts and Entertainment: The Third Mountain of Influence

As with media, the world of arts and entertainment holds great sway over people. We take in movies, television shows, books, paintings, and other forms of art and entertainment daily, and this area of life is meant to be a blessing and inspiration for us. It is meant to portray the beauty of what God has made, His goodness, and the value system He has provided for our benefit. Yet often, so much of what is shared is not uplifting.

We can pray for godly people to rise up as influencers for good in arts and entertainment. We can pray for those who are artists and entertainers to come into a relationship with the Lord. As they do, their creative work will reflect what is good and godly and be a blessing to many.

Divine influence can happen in many ways. For instance, I have a son who is a professional music composer for many purposes, including video games. He is also a Christian. I am so blessed listening to the beautiful instrumental music he is writing as the soundtrack for various games, because I can hear the hand of the Lord in it.

Even if we do not personally hold a career in arts and entertainment, we can make good, godly choices in what we will allow into our lives. We can evaluate this by asking ourselves, "Is what I am seeing and hearing drawing me closer to the Lord, or pushing me farther away from Him?" If it is not inspiring us in godly ways, then we must make a decision about whether we will allow it to remain in our life.

For those of us who create art or entertainment in any way, even in our personal blogs or things we do for ourselves and share on social media, we should be mindful of allowing those creations to show forth the glory and beauty and love of God. The Bible tells us that what we share with the world should not be a "stumbling block" to others (2 Corinthians 6:3; Romans 14:13), so that we do not make them doubt God because of what they see in us. If it is something God would not portray in heaven, then it is not something we should portray on earth.

Business: The Fourth Mountain of Influence

This mountain of influence is very important to our lives, because without finances, none of the other mountains can grow. Finances are essential to every area of life, and God desires us to have sufficiency so that we can enjoy our lives and be free to accomplish all He has called us to do. Thus, having godly people in the business sphere is crucial.

One way that we are called to be an influence here is through prayer. And we can pray that godly men and women will rise to the top in business, becoming CEOs and leaders who are led by the Lord's direction in their decision-making. We can come into agreement with the Lord about having godly people in positions where they can create successful companies and bring in economic blessings to their employees. We can believe for those in leadership positions to pour wealth into God's Kingdom, so that it can grow and bless others even more.

In addition to praying for business leaders, we can pray for ourselves to be a godly influence in the business realm. I say this because the majority of us will become involved in business in some way. Most people hold a job at some point in their lives, and even when those positions are temporary or part-time, we still have opportunities to be a positive godly influence.

For those of us who work full-time in a business career or who own a company, we must remember that our godly values matter. As we walk with the Lord and allow Him to lead us in following godly values in our business, the wealth we may desire to have will follow. Those values must come first!

How do those values come forth in our work and career? We can seek the Lord and stay connected to Him. When we are connected to the vine (Jesus), we will bear fruit (John chapter 15). As we remain close to Him, He can guide us and help us to be a blessing to others through our business. And as we do so, we shall be blessed in return with finances to meet our needs and so much more. Wealth is a by-product of our relationship with God, and as we stay connected to Him, our businesses will be blessed.

We can also choose to support businesses that pursue godly purposes. We can stand with them by spending at those businesses, and by choosing not to spend in places where we know the leaders are not following godly principles and values.

Education: The Fifth Mountain of Influence

The future of our nation depends on our children, and our children are taught what to value not only at home, but in our schools. For this reason, the values and principles being taught in our educational system are crucial to this country's success. And our children's own success in life is tied to what they learn as well.

As with the other mountains of influence, our prayers of faith are important. We can pray for godly teachers, school administrators, and other school leaders to be set into place so that they can stand up for what is godly in our educational systems. We can pray for every level of the educational system, from preschool and kindergarten all the way through college. Whatever age your child may be right now, you can pray for godly instructors and godly classmates to be in their lives to provide a positive influence, and for your children to be a godly influence for others.

Beyond the school system, it's important to realize that there are many other ways that education is offered, and it comes to us at all ages. Whether it is through self-help books, websites that provide health information, coaching and classes, or other areas of education taught in places such as senior centers, and so many other places, we are being educated all the time. We can expand our prayers to encompass these areas as well.

Even when we are not purposely serving in a teaching career, we all find ourselves in situations where we have an opportunity to instruct others. It may be some informal coaching we provide to a new employee that we work with. It may be in a church setting as a volunteer, teaching other adults, or training other volunteers. It may be at home as we show our children a new skill. We, too, are educators in our own way.

Because teachers can have such a strong guiding influence on others, God holds them to a higher standard. So, for those of us who teach, it is vital that we ensure we are following the Lord closely and bringing every area of our lives to Him so that He can point out anything that is questionable or unlike Him that we need to repent of and change. We must be beyond reproach.

Religion: The Sixth Mountain of Influence

Our religious freedom is at risk in today's world, and it is key that we stand strong in our belief in Jesus Christ and in our Christian values. To do so, we must know what God's Word says, so that we can bring these godly principles into our spheres of influence. It is important to take time to read the Bible, study it, meditate on it, and pray so that we can be a godly force for good in this world.

If we look around the world, we see many places where people have lost their religious freedom. In many nations, it is not safe for people to worship the Lord Jesus. In our nation, we have the freedom to worship as we choose, but we must not take this for granted. It is a right we must defend. Being free to believe is our God given right and has an impact in every area of life, not just for ourselves but for others.

If we stand aside and do not speak up against that which is wrong, then we are party to what is happening. We have a responsibility for what we do and don't do. When we have the power and opportunity to speak up, we must do so!

There are many ways that we can speak up for our religious freedom such as standing up for free speech, staying informed and voting on legislation that protects our religious freedoms, and practicing your religious freedom by being unashamed and prepared to share the Gospel. We do this to help maintain a country that is free, blessed and filled with goodness. In this way, as our country remains free, we can be an influence for good on the rest of the world. Remember, we are called to make disciples. We cannot do so if we are not protecting our freedom to share Jesus with others. But as we stand up for what is right, we can be a shining light that draws people closer to the Lord.

Those of us in positions within a religious organization or ministry should take these stances very seriously. Pastors, teachers, and church staff—whether paid or volunteer—must continue to be a good witness, and practice fully their religious rights, upholding great standards, and setting the example on the influence of religion, making sure not to be a stumbling block to anyone within their sphere of influence.

Family: The Seventh Mountain of Influence

The final mountain of influence is the family—which is the bedrock for all the other pillars of influence that I have mentioned. This area of life is usually not associated with our career, but it most certainly is a ministry—and a vital one!

There are so many ways that the word "family" is defined these days. Our responsibility as believers in Christ is to apply what we know from His Word and stand for godly values in families. The guide for what constitutes a family in the eyes of God is found in His Word. Scriptures such as Genesis 2:18, Genesis 2:24, and others make it clear that God views the family unit as consisting of a man and a woman—one husband and one wife.

At times, because we live in a fallen world where our lives do not go as planned, a divorce may occur, and a single parent may be raising a child. You may come to know the Lord after having a child outside of wedlock. You may be married yet have no children. The Lord has grace for you in your family situation.

Ultimately, God desires us to honor Him in our family. Joshua 24:15 says, "As for me and my household, we will serve the Lord." Whether you are a parent, a spouse, or a single person, or you are a mentor for others providing a family-type influence, worship and honor God. God calls us to serve Him in the midst of our families, showing forth what is good and godly so that we can lead our family members to the Lord.

The family is the center of so much of our lives, and it is no wonder that it is under such attack these days. The devil wants to kill, steal, and destroy (John 10:10), and the first place he will attack is the family. He knows that if he can disrupt and divide our families, he can distract us and cause us to slide back from our influence in other spheres of life.

As Christians, we must stand up against attacks on our family. We must pray and work toward peace and unity in our family, standing against the divisions that the devil is trying to create. Relationships are the number one area that the enemy can use to disrupt us, so this area is so key to our success.

We cannot control others, but we can always choose what is good and godly for ourselves. Choosing God and serving Him will bring His blessings into your home.

Our Mountains of Influence Have Seasons

Just as we may have more than one mountain of influence where we hold a role, we may find that our roles may change over time. In the past, perhaps you worked part-time but now you work full-time, or vice-versa. Or maybe you are a stay-at-home parent now while your child is an infant, but you have plans to return to business in a few years when your child begins to attend school. Seasons come and go, and the Lord desires to lead us into making changes when it is time to do so.

Oftentimes, we can have a job that we once loved, but now we know it is no longer a fit for us, and we become ready to make a change. This can be very good for us if we navigate it wisely. We all shift and change, and there are times when we are called to a specific job or workplace. It is important to pray about the timing and purpose to make sure we are where we are supposed to be. Go to the Lord and seek His wisdom and direction. He will reveal to you where you are supposed to be.

In my own life, I was a hairstylist for many years. But as I aged, I found that the work was simply too hard on my body. At the same time, I faced difficulties in my marriage. I began to seek the Lord, asking questions, and looking for His purpose for me. As I sought Him and allowed Him to help me think outside of the box, I found myself drawn to the work I do now: Christian coaching.

Ask yourself, what is true? What do you need to do? What is the plan? What goals do you want to set, and for what purpose? What will success look like, and how will you give back once you have achieved that success?

The seasons of our career and ministry positions shift and change over time, and this is a natural part of life. As these seasons change, we often move our position on our mountains of influence, and it is good to recognize these shifts and embrace them as the Lord would have us do. Remember, as with all things, awareness is key! As we are aware of these changes as they arise, we can make better decisions about what to do next.

As old doors may close and as new opportunities arise, be willing to learn new skills, make changes as God directs, and adapt to your new season. God desires to help us move forward into our new season. Be secure in knowing that whatever may be shifting, you are not stuck! Even if you have held the same career for a long time, you are not stuck there. There are many classes you can take, and many opportunities to grow and move into another career if you desire to do so.

Sometimes when we feel a need to shift, it doesn't automatically mean we must change our career. Seek the Lord because He may have you in your specific job for a reason. You are making an income there, and you may be needed as a positive influence. If the Lord still desires you to be in that position, then your desire to do something else may mean that you should seek an outlet in another area, such as a new hobby or a volunteer opportunity that allows you to explore your interests and pursue your godly purpose.

Be encouraged! Even when disappointments come up, you don't have to remain stuck in that place. Get up and seek the information, education, and other resources you need to be successful. Everything you need, God will give to you. Seek His direction every single day for as long as it takes to get into the new position He has for you. You will have great peace, contentment, and fulfillment in your sphere of influence as you allow God to direct and equip you in your career and ministry.

Day 1

Career and Ministry
Work for the Lord

*"Put your heart and soul into every activity you do,
as though you are doing it for the Lord himself and not merely for others.
For we know that we will receive a reward, an inheritance from the Lord,
as we serve the Lord Yahweh, the Anointed One!"*
—Colossians 3:23–24 (TPT)

Maintaining a good attitude toward work is so helpful in preserving your emotional well-being. Whatever you may do throughout the day—whether you are at a job, working at home, helping family, serving at church, caring for your property, or any other form of "labor"—do it with the Lord in mind. Consider how you can show forth His light in every situation, and know that He is your rewarder and the Source of your blessings.

Gain Insight

Answer the questions, be honest with yourself and be transformed!

1. In what ways can you work as if working for the Lord? Explain.

2. Does your attitude matter when working?

3. Are you different when no one is looking? In what ways?

4. How does Jesus serve others, and in what ways can you emulate Him?

5. Do others see Jesus in you at work and ministry? In what ways?

Pray

Thank You, Lord, that You have given me an example of how to work and serve You. Help me to have great self-control and to treat others better than myself, even when I am tired. Help me to trust that You see, and You provide. I know You will open doors for me and bless me as I continue to work as if working for You!

Day 2

Career and Ministry
Seek God's Advice

"I hear the Lord saying, 'I will stay close to you,
instructing and guiding you along the pathway for your life.
I will advise you along the way
and lead you forth with my eyes as your guide.
So don't make it difficult; don't be stubborn
when I take you where you've not been before.
Don't make me tug you and pull you along.
Just come with me!'"
—**Psalm 32:8–9 (TPT)**

God is so good and so caring about the details of our lives that He desires to lead us even in the details of our career, ministry, service to others and every mountain of influence. Remember our principle, "You Know It!" This means you know in your heart what He has created you to do, and He desires to bring that knowledge to the forefront of your mind so that you can accomplish His purposes, enjoy working and serving others, and be blessed!

Gain Insight

Answer the questions, be honest with yourself and be transformed!

1. What questions would you like to ask God about your career, ministry, and other roles in which you serve others?

2. What would you like to do if you could do anything?

3. Do you need to take extra training?

4. What do you feel God is calling you to do?

5. Who here on earth is healthy that you can process this information with?

Pray

Thank You, Lord, that You guide and direct my path, that You will give me wisdom concerning my career choices. I am so grateful to know that You long to see me succeed. Help me to seek You each and every step of the way. I know You will bless the hard work that I do and that You will help me to prosper.

Day 3

Career and Ministry
Use Your Talents

*"Every believer has received grace gifts, so use them to serve one another
as faithful stewards of the many-colored tapestry of God's grace.
For example, if you have a speaking gift, speak as though God were speaking
his words through you. If you have the gift of serving, do it passionately
with the strength God gives you, so that in everything God alone
will be glorified through Jesus Christ. For to him belong the power
and the glory forever throughout all ages! Amen."*
—1 Peter 4:10–11 (TPT)

God has provided each of us with unique gifts and talents that we can tap into and use to make a living while also adding value to those around us. He also gives us creativity and insights into ways we can use the skills we have, as well as ideas for skills we can go out and gain, in order to be successful in our career, ministry, and anywhere else we have influence. As you take time to seek Him, you can expect to see how these talents and skills can be used for His glory and to the benefit of yourself and those around you.

Gain Insight

Answer the questions, be honest with yourself and be transformed!

1. What talents or skills do you currently possess?

2. Do you believe you can increase your skills and talents? In what way?

3. Who needs the skills that you possess?

   _____
   _____
   _____

4. How do your skills further the kingdom of God?

   _____
   _____
   _____

5. Would God be proud of what you are doing? In what ways?

   _____
   _____
   _____

Pray

Thank You, Lord, for giving me skills and talents. Help me to continue to develop more skills to serve others and give glory to Your name! Give me wisdom as to where to spend my time and money developing my skills. Help me to understand the needs of others so I can be of great benefit to them and further succeed in my career, ministry, and serving others because of it. Bless all that I do for Your kingdom, Lord.

Day 4

Career and Ministry
Passion and Joy

*"Because of you, I know the path of life,
as I taste the fullness of joy in your presence.
At your right I experience divine pleasures forevermore!"*
—**Psalm 16:11 (TPT)**

The joy of the Lord is such a wonderful gift! There is to be fullness of joy in all we do, including our career and ministry. As we become aware of what we are passionate about, we can seek ways to do the work we love to do. And being about the business that God has created us to do breeds such joy and delight. What an amazing way to live!

Gain Insight

Answer the questions, be honest with yourself and be transformed!

1. What passions has God placed on your heart?

2. Do you believe God desires a good life for you? In what ways?

3. What area of need in the world has God made you passionate about?

4. What will bring great joy into your life?

5. Do you believe that God desires you to be passionate and joy-filled? In what ways?

Pray

Thank You, Lord, that You desire a wild, passionate journey for me in my life! You make life exciting! Help me to feel the passion that You have for me so I can be passionate toward others. Fill my life with Your joy! Fill me with energy and a burning desire to bring the Good News of the Gospel to others through all that I do to serve them! Thank You, Lord, that You care about how I feel! More and more of You, Lord, is what I desire! Thank You, Jesus, for filling my cup to overflowing so I can fill the cups of others.

Day 5

Career and Ministry
Awareness and Belief

*"I tell you this timeless truth:
The person who follows me in faith, believing in me,
will do the same mighty miracles that I do—even greater miracles
than these because I go to be with my Father!"*
—**John 14:12 (TPT)**

As we serve others through our jobs, our daily labors for those in our lives, and any volunteering we may do, we can show forth the heart of God, just as Jesus did as He was about His Father's business during His time of ministry. The Holy Spirit empowers us to do this, and we can draw on His strength, His guidance, and His insights to be successful as we work as unto the Lord.

Gain Insight

Answer the questions, be honest with yourself and be transformed!

1. How does being aware of the Holy Spirit in your life affect your belief that you can do anything?

2. What would you have the power of the Holy Spirit do for you in your life?

3. In what ways can you become more aware of the needs of others?

4. What are some of the things you can do for others with the help and power of the Holy Spirit?

5. What steps can you take to believe more in the power of the Holy Spirit?

Pray

Thank You, Lord Jesus, that You have given me great authority and power in Your name! Help me to become more and more aware of what the Holy Spirit can do in my life and in the lives of others. Help me to see the needs of others and to know I have the ability to make a difference in their lives. Help me to use my God-given power in a way that is pleasing to You, Lord Jesus. Let all that I do glorify You and bring healing and relief to others.

Day 6

Career and Ministry
Seasons

"He changes times and seasons; he removes kings and sets up kings; he gives wisdom to the wise and knowledge to those who have understanding."
—**Daniel 2:21 (ESV)**

For everything in life, there is a season, and this is true of our work, ministry, and other roles we hold to. We can be led of the Lord in decisions concerning our careers and service, including when it is time to look for a new job, when it is time to stay at home or work less so we have more time to care for loved ones, and when to retire. As we seek the Lord, He can show us ahead of time when seasons in our life are about to change, and He can give us insights for what to do next.

Gain Insight

Answer the questions, be honest with yourself and be transformed!

1. What are some of the different jobs (roles) you have had in your life?

2. What did the different jobs (roles) teach you?

3. In what ways can you seek God's help when you feel it is time to change careers?

4. What are some of the signs you will know when it is time to change?

5. How will you plan to care for your needs during times of change?

Pray

Lord, thank You for giving me the wisdom and discernment I need when it comes to changing careers or moving into a new role in ministry or other areas of serving. Thank You for helping me to plan for my needs and those You have placed in my care when I need to make changes. Help me to seek godly counsel to make sure the changes I make are beneficial to myself and my family. Thank You for providing change and new opportunities to serve You, Lord.

Day 7

Career and Ministry
Rest

"Are you weary, carrying a heavy burden? Come to me.
I will refresh your life, for I am your oasis. Simply join your life with mine.
Learn my ways and you'll discover that I'm gentle, humble, easy to please.
You will find refreshment and rest in me.
For all that I require of you will be pleasant and easy to bear."
—Matthew 11:28–30 (TPT)

Just as with the other areas of life, the sphere of our career and ministry is to be balanced between times of labor and times to rest and be refreshed. Rather than giving into the world's tendency to glorify working all the time, let God show you when to work, when to rest, and when to take time for other areas of life such as exercise and time for your relationships. In this way, you can achieve better balance.

Gain Insight

Answer the questions, be honest with yourself and be transformed!

1. Resting from work involves our minds as well as our bodies. In what ways are you able to turn off your mind?

2. In what ways can you establish a time to work and a time to rest? Write down your schedule.

3. What can you do before bed to make sure you turn off thoughts of work?

4. What can you visualize to give you great peace concerning work?

5. What can you let others know so they can support your need for rest?

Pray

Lord, help me to set aside work in both my body and my mind so that I can be refreshed and serve others well. Help me to let go of the day and trust in your provision for both work and income. Thank You, Lord, for the permission to rest. Give me great vision of Your provision and a great hope for my future. Thank You, Jesus, for all that You do for me. Help me to emulate You in all that I do.

Reflection for the Week on Career and Ministry

Answer the questions, be honest with yourself and be transformed!

1. Are you moving closer to your career and ministry goals?

2. Is there anything getting in the way?

3. Do you need to set any new plans?

4. Have you found an accountability partner?

5. In what ways can you help someone in their career and ministry?

Week Six: Career and Ministry

Write Your Inner Narration

Using what you have learned from this chapter, the scriptures you have memorized this week, and what you discovered while answering this week's questions, build on your original narration from weeks 1, 2, 3, 4, and 5, and write an additional short godly narration using only positive words. If you find it helpful, review your answers to the daily questions from this week, take note of any positive words, and include them in your new godly narration for this week.

Example: I AM beautiful. I AM loved by God, just as I AM.
I AM forgiven. I AM pleasing to God. I AM strong. I AM courageous.

I AM filled with godly purpose. I AM equipped and able to achieve my godly goals.
I AM a son or a daughter of the King. I AM covered in His grace.
Nothing anyone says or does can harm me because I AM protected.

I AM healthy in my boundaries. I AM forgiving. I AM loved in my relationships.
I AM wise and gracious in my interactions with others in my life.

I AM emotionally well, I AM focused. I AM at peace and rested. I AM balanced.
I AM aware of what I feel and I AM led by God in how to respond to my emotions.

I AM strong in my body. I AM led by God in what to eat and drink for my health and well-being.
I make time for exercise and rest because I AM caring for my body, which is the temple of the Holy Spirit.

I AM passionate about fulfilling God's purpose in my career and/or ministry.
I AM filled with purpose and focus as I work and volunteer my time.
I AM equipped to be successful in my job... etc.

Week Seven

Finances

Our finances will either give us the life we desire or will hamper every area of our life because of lack. The good news is that God cares about your financial wellness. He desires to help you manage and improve your finances so that you will not only experience joy as your needs are met, but also so you can bless the lives of others and further His kingdom through great causes. Poor financial management can lead to many problems. But wise financial choices can create many benefits in every area.

The content and blessed life is not so much about how much income you have, but how you manage your income and thus build even more. The principles we have applied to the other areas of our life are applicable here as well. Remember each area overlaps, so as one area improves, the other areas improve as well. This is true in finances too; as you improve financially, all the other areas of your life will improve as well.

When things aren't going well financially, it affects how we feel emotionally. The stress we feel over finances can affect our physical health, and spill over into our relationships, causing stress there, as well as the other areas. So, managing our financial life with godly wisdom is vital to our overall well-being and to gaining freedom and transformation in this important area of life.

Gaining Financial Freedom

Financial freedom starts with trusting the Lord with this area of your life. When you know and have complete faith in the Lord as your source, He will meet your every need. This is so important to alleviating the fear and stress that can arise around finances.

What does it mean for God to meet your need? It means He will direct you in the way you should go to earn an income. Sometimes, we think or have been taught that God will miraculously provide for us without our doing anything. And sometimes, people do bless us at God's prompting. An unexpected check may arrive in the mail, or someone may bless you with some cash or a gift card. And yes, these unexpected blessings can and should be enjoyed.

But it's important to understand that this kind of miraculous, unexpected provision is not the primary way for God to meet your needs. Instead, He desires to provide you with wisdom, energy, and open doors to supply your need. To gain that direction, you must go to the Lord in prayer and spend time with Him diligently to gain understanding from Him regarding your work, income, wealth, finances, your budget and more.

As you consistently do this, He will instruct you on what to do. He will point you to the classes you need, or the ideas for your business, or the people in your industry that you can speak to as you pursue your career. He will provide the answers and insights that fit you and your situation and help you to fulfill your purpose.

Remember, too, that God is not limited by the supply at hand. Don't let fear over how the economy looks deter you or intimidate you. His supply is limitless, and He will give you creativity and direct you where you need to go in order to tap into that supply at any given time.

Good Financial Management Begins with Our Beliefs

Our understanding and beliefs pertaining to finances matter greatly. The world offers many distorted views and beliefs about money. The misconceptions about the purpose of money and wealth have caused much damage in many lives. Some of us may have been taught that money is the only thing in life that matters, or that the only way to "protect" ourselves is to gain more and more wealth. Or, we may have come to believe that money is evil, or that being wealthy means you're not spiritual. Most have not been taught proper money management and thus have had failures in managing their money, causing them to think that they will always be "bad" at finances.

Such belief systems impact how we view and thus operate in our financial life. As Christians, we have been given great wisdom concerning wealth in the scriptures. God has a powerful, eye-opening view on money, and as you take on His perspective, you will prosper. God sees people first, above all, and we too can take this perspective. God does not judge people for their wealth or their poverty; instead, he values the person. As we learn how to value people and offer value to their lives through our talents and skills, our business and our finances will naturally increase.

God loves us no matter how much money we have, or how much we don't have. He loves us no matter where we are at in our finances right now. And He also desires to see us thrive and be transformed. He cares about our decisions around finances because they reflect the beliefs within us and the values that we are adhering to. Our financial decisions reflect what is in our hearts and minds.

As we live consistently with His Word and His purpose for our lives, we will prosper. The Lord desires us to enjoy our lives and to do good in the world, which becomes more and more possible when we have abundance in our lives to share with others.

In other words, financial success is a good thing, as long as you use what you have been given to honor the Lord!

As you begin reprogramming your mind to use money to bless people, instead of using people to gain money, you will find you are more and more blessed. The love of money is where problem lies. If we love money more than God and others, and trust in our wealth instead of God, then there will be issues that arise that are not for our good.

But as we trust in the Lord to provide for us and put Him first, we can find it easier to make good decisions concerning our finances—including what to save, what to spend, and what to give. This allows us to prosper, so that we can have an abundant life filled with more than enough to meet our needs.

Remember this—money is just an object, but our relationship with it is key, because it can help us to fulfill our purpose. Much good can be done to bless others and further God's Kingdom when we sow financial gifts in the right places, as God leads us. Having the money to not only meet our own needs but to give to others is a blessing, as it helps us to do the work of God's Kingdom on the earth.

> *"Give generously and generous gifts will be given back to you,*
> *shaken down to make room for more.*
> *Abundant gifts will pour out upon you with*
> *such an overflowing measure that it will run over the top!*
> *The measurement of your generosity becomes the measurement of your return."*
> **—Luke 6:38 (TPT)**

As you connect with God and begin to understand your finances, you will learn to sow your seeds in a way that blesses others and also brings about the harvest of blessings that God intends for you.

What Money Really Is

Let's take a look at what money really is, so that any wrong or limiting beliefs may be broken. Money is energy.

Long ago, before there were dollar bills or banks, people exchanged services or traded goods. They expended their energy to create something, and as a result, they gained something in return. Today, if you use your energy and work for someone, you are given a wage. If you trade products or services, this is an exchange of energy as well. You are able to produce a harvest because of the energy you've given to yield that produce.

Let me say it again: Money is energy! It empowers us to trade what we have for what we need. It allows us to use the energy we have within us to be productive in the world. You provide a service, you give of your energy, and you reap the reward in finances.

As you begin thinking about money not as bills and coins, but as a force that produces things, you will begin to transform your finances because you will direct your energy toward producing results with the energy you expend. Therefore, it is important to gain an understanding on how to use your energy to leverage the skills and talents you have to bless others. This will produce your financial harvest.

How God Views Money

To be transformed in our finances, let's look more closely at how God views the purpose of money and finances. To begin, realize that our use of money is to be rooted in our spiritual relationship with the Lord. It starts with honoring God, taking care of our family and self, supporting God's Kingdom, and adding value to other people. The Bible says that when we are connected to the vine, we will bear fruit (see John chapter 15). This is true not only in the spiritual arena, but in other areas as well, including our finances.

When we add value to people's lives, we bear fruit. There's a natural energy that happens there. It is God's law. When you add value, you will reap a harvest through what you have sown.

As you consider what you'd like to sow and what you value, ask yourself: What do you believe about God and money? Your answer is going to determine the direction and outcome of your finances, especially for Christians who desire to live according to what God's Word says.

For me personally, I believe God hates poverty. Let me be clear—He does not hold anything against the people who struggle with it. He loves people, no matter how much money they have or lack. But the condition of poverty itself is terrible, and it leads to so many challenges and suffering. And I believe God sent Jesus to free us from it!

Look at how poverty affects people. It does horrible things to people and puts them in terrible, heartbreaking situations. It prevents them from living their lives fully and hinders their ability to gain and use their skills and talents in ways that bless others, because they must concentrate instead on survival from day to day. When people struggle with having a safe place to eat and sleep, it limits much of what they are able to accomplish. As we work to help others break free from poverty in both circumstances and mindset, they can grow in their ability to thrive and to serve the Lord.

"Those who live to bless others will have blessings heaped upon them,
and the one who pours out his life to pour out blessings will be saturated with favor."
—Proverbs 11:25 (TPT)

We are all designed to increase our wealth and generously give—to love God and love others. He desires us to bless others.

This is why I believe we are to partner with God and help meet the needs of others. As Christians, we are not victims! We can rise up and make an income, help others in need and break the chains of poverty! It is best to not give a handout, but to give a hand-up, so that those who are blessed can rise up and be a blessing too. We are all called to be a blessing, and financial wholeness helps to put us in a position where we can successfully, effectively do that. That is God's best for us.

God Desires to Bless You Financially

God gave you the ability, the energy, the health, the intellect and all the other tools you need to work and make an income so you can be a blessing. This is His desire for your life—that you would be productive and make an income to provide for your needs and that of your family, and also be able to give when He calls you to give.

There are others who have no need of an income from their skills, and therefore consider the work they do as service or ministry. They may have no desire for a financial reward. And that's fine too; the work is the reward (the harvest) in itself because they desire to do ministry and have the means to do so.

But make no mistake. It is also acceptable and permissible to bring in an income by adding value to other people's lives. That's what we want to do as Christians—we want to bring value to others and ourselves and therefore earn an income in a way that is pleasing to the Lord.

Finding a place of balance in this area is key. Without balance, we may find ourselves giving our energy without receiving back what we need, and that is not God's plan for us. I've worked with many people in my coaching business who have given so much of their time and giftings to ministry, yet they felt they didn't have a right to earn an income from their work. They feel as if they are helping people, and so they shouldn't accept payment for their work. As a result, they have little to nothing left over for their personal needs. This often overlaps into their emotional life, and they become bitter, which then overlaps into their spiritual life, impacting their relationship with God.

And all the while, God's best for them was that they use their skills He gave to them to earn money and have their needs met through the value added to others. Yes, we all have been commissioned to bring others to the Lord, and some of us do that through a formal ministry. We all should find ways to give back and be a blessing. But we are also called to take the needed care of ourselves and our families.

This blurring of what is acceptable in the area of finances and ministry is where confusion can begin to happen. This is where time and money management come into play, so you can determine what will be the source of your income, and what will be considered charity.

God has given us the ability to govern our lives and make wise decisions on where we will spend our time, talents, and income for His kingdom. There is a proper order to how we are to manage our lives. We are to manage our homes, and we do that through income and provision. We would be living out of balance if we tried to provide for others before ourselves and our families. Once we have that area of our finances in order, we can then extend our time, money, and talents out to others.

Remember, God has told us if we are faithful with little, we will be faithful with much. As we continue managing the little we have been blessed with, we will continue to increase. We must draw a line and decide where to put our energy for each of these areas of life. Even if we don't need money, we still must determine where to put our time and resources. And even if we already have money, it is not wrong to desire to earn more if there is a purpose involved in it.

I am grateful for the blessing to be able to offer my time, talents, and finances in ministry. Even still, I believe it is appropriate that those who receive the value offered through classes, membership and private coaching services pay for those services so that I can reach even more people and offer these same services to those who are in need of healing, as well as restoring lives by offering resources to other charities. So for me, I manage my time and finances by deciding what is a paid income and what is charitable.

I believe this pleases the Lord and furthers His kingdom, and it allows others the opportunity to partner with me financially and glorify the Lord. I encourage you to take a similar approach. Ask Him to show you where to earn your income for daily living and let Him guide you in where to give your time, talents and income as a charitable blessing.

Seek God's Wisdom for Your Finances

*"And if anyone longs to be wise, ask God for wisdom and he will give it!
He won't see your lack of wisdom as an opportunity to scold you over your
failures, but he will overwhelm your failures with his generous grace."*
—**James 1:5 (TPT)**

God loves wisdom and knowledge, and His desire is for you to increase in skill so you can gain the information you need to prosper. God appreciates intelligence and education. There are countries around the world that do the opposite—they prevent children from going to school and keep them ignorant. This is against the design God has established. Knowledge and wisdom are of the Lord.

When it comes to finances, there are many ways we can lean on God's wisdom to guide us. Have you invested your time to learn what you need to know about how to make money?

For example, there are so many ways to use our time and skills to provide for ourselves. Some people grow crops and sell them. Some offer services. Some create art. All these things can bring in income. It is up to us to decide where our energy goes so that we put the proper amount of that energy into generating finances.

Take time to pray and seek the Lord, so that He can guide you about how to make your income. Let Him guide you in how to learn the needed skills and where to apply for a job. Remember, He desires us to seek Him for the wisdom on what to do, where to go, and what classes to take to gain the knowledge we need to earn an income. Ask Him what you need to do and what information you need to gain.

Remember, your experiences in life contribute to what you do to earn money. So, whatever God has placed on your heart to do, go learn the skills and knowledge you need to do it with success.

Another area where God can provide you with wisdom in the management of your income is through having a budget. Know that God desires for you to manage your money well. If you start to gain wealth yet don't know how to wisely manage your money, you will become like the person who started off rich but lost it all.

One of the most practical things you can do to manage your money is to have your eyes on it and be organized. A budget is excellent for this, as it helps you identify a clear purpose for your money, and also helps you to stay balanced in your income and spending. Today, there are so many tools and apps you can use to manage your money and watch your budget. With them, you can set up protocols and rules for where money goes when it comes into your hands. Keep in mind that your money will quietly disappear if you are not aware. Set goals and plans for your money and where it will go.

It's important to set boundaries on your finances. This is what having a budget is—a set of boundaries that guides your investments and spending. You can and should actively choose what you will spend money on, and what you will limit or avoid spending money on. These guidelines and rules established for yourself are essential to allowing your finances to grow over time.

The number one thing to know about budget is awareness. Keep track of your money by writing down what you make, what your expenses are, set aside 10% to tithe, 10% savings and live on the remaining 80%. This is the 10-10-80 rule that my family and I live by. As we have increased in finances, we've created other accounts for further investments as well as accounts for our children and their educations. It is important to learn what to do with your money as it grows and increases.

If you need more one-on-one time with someone to help you budget, you can take classes; there are churches that offer them for free. There are plenty of resources available to you if you will simply seek and become aware. Ask the Holy Spirit to help you learn and understand what to do so that you will be in better charge of your finances.

Whatever it is you need to know about finances, let Him lead you to the right source of information to help you grow. This is a part of transforming your financial life.

Money and You

Since you have now become clear on God's view on finances, continue to examine your mindset and become aware of anything that is not in harmony with His perspective. Begin by asking yourself these questions concerning your beliefs.

What do you believe about finances? Do you believe that you are capable of building wealth? Or do you believe that there are some who are just lucky, but you're not one of them? Do you see budgeting as a way to ensure your bills are paid and your savings are growing, or do you think of it as confusing, restrictive, or "no fun?"

Do you believe that you are wise enough to manage your wealth? If you don't have the knowledge you need right now, do you believe that you can go out and learn it? Or do you tend to tell yourself you "just can't figure out" how to handle money?

What do you believe about how money should be managed in a household? Do you believe it has to be the husband (or the wife) who handles it? Do you feel like it has to be you because you don't trust anyone with your money? Are you willing to allow your spouse to handle the money? Or perhaps you believe it is best for you both to share the financial duties?

Remember, awareness of your mindset and beliefs is key to transformation. To gain this awareness, ask yourself: Are there any areas in your life where you were taught lies about God, yourself, and wealth? What was spoken to you in your home as you were growing up? What did you learn that was not true?

In my childhood, I grew up in a family where there was extreme dysfunction around money management. My parents did not manage money well; they falsely believed they were capable of managing money, yet there was never a budget, and they never learned skills about money management. Additionally, they had a poverty mindset, and would say things like, "Only the wealthy survive. It takes money to make money, and we don't have money."

Remember when I said that money is energy? It doesn't take money to make money; it takes energy to make money. The truth is that we all have energy; it is something God has given us. So, we already have what we need to make money. What I learned growing up was wrong. But as I gained awareness of the truth in this area, it has freed me to earn an income in ways I would never have anticipated growing up.

If we are going to become prosperous and effective at making and increasing money, we need to consider how we see ourselves and how we feel about ourselves. If you've been wounded in some way and have not yet processed it and found healing, the wound may manifest in how you handle your finances.

Sometimes, these wounds can lead people to spend on selfish or unfruitful things, such as alcohol or on gambling away the rent money. It can also lead to the kind of poverty mentality that my parents displayed. It's important to gain healing so that you can think clearly about money and manage it wisely.

What new mindset do you need to gain? Where do you need to increase in knowledge? Be honest with yourself, as the truth will set you free. The fruits of your income and life don't lie, so look around and notice what is true about you. Then, begin to really seek the wisdom found in the Lord. Look at your experiences and skills. Ask God for more and more wisdom and He will give it to you!

When we honor God by making sure that our mindset around money lines up with His way of seeing it, then we will find it easier to align ourselves with His will. It will then be easier to value our energy, earn an income, manage our money, and spend wisely.

Achieving Balance in the Area of Finances

There are many misconceptions we can come to believe about wealth. But what I personally have seen to be true is that wealth is a blessing, a tool we can use to help people as God intended. When people are struggling financially, it tends to overlap into their spiritual life, causing people to become bitter and feel like God doesn't care. So, financial wellness is a gift that can strengthen our spiritual connection to the Lord. This means it is something we can seek with the Lord's help and guidance so that we handle our finances in a way that is pleasing to Him.

Partner with the Lord and ask Him for wisdom and guidance in the area of making decisions about your time, talents and finances. He has given you the ability and freedom to govern your life, and He will help direct your path when you seek His wisdom. Use your freedom and self-control in a way that pleases Him. As you create more wealth, you will need more wisdom to discern where to spend your time and energy as more charitable opportunities become available to you.

God is a productive God, and a God of order and organization. He is balanced as He also knows how to rest. He desires to help us become more like Him as we schedule and order our day so that we are blessed and cared for. It is important for us to seek God for wisdom so that He can bless us with order, balance, fulfillment, purpose, and provision. This is especially true in helping us to keep our finances, our work life, our giving, and our personal lives in order.

"To everything there is a season,
a time for every purpose under heaven."
—Ecclesiastes 3:1 (NKJV)

There's a season for enjoying yourself, for relaxing and taking a vacation. There's a season for taking care of your own needs and the things you desire to have in your life. There is a season and time that you go and do charity work for people and volunteer. God will give you the wisdom you need for each season financially as you create and manage your life according to His good guidance.

Elijah is an excellent example of this need for balance. He did great ministry work in defeating the prophets of Baal on Mount Carmel (1 Kings 18). But afterward, he needed rest and refreshing. He needed nourishment and self-care. He needed time away with God so that God could refuel him. Once he took that valuable time for refreshing, he was able to do more for the Lord.

As you contemplate this area, know that balance in the area of finance looks different for everyone. What is best for you will not be the same as it is for others, and it is good to discern the difference. Someone who is living in a tent doing missions may be in balance, or out of balance, depending on God's plan for them. And it is the same with someone living in a beautiful home with a great career. Balance isn't determined by financial wealth, ministry, or outward things you may have or lack. It is determined by what God's will is for you personally.

You and God know the answer that fits you. When you're out of sync with His plan for you, you'll know. As you seek Him, He will tell you when to give, what to donate, what to save, and how to manage your budget. He will show you what to balance in your career, your ministry, and your finances, so that you can live a life of abundance and joy in Him.

Develop a Giving Heart

As with every other area of life, we are not meant to simply hold onto everything we have. We are meant to give. As we give, we make room for an increase. This is a divine cycle, to give as you receive. Continue to ask God for wisdom on where to give your energy in order to receive. As you do, keep a thankful heart and give Him all honor, glory and praise.

As you continue in gratitude for the Lord you will have more energy to go out and earn more money. The more energy you have, the more you will be able to increase. A lack of gratitude creates the opposite effect, draining us of energy and impeding our ability to grow. Our attitude is so important. As you anchor yourself in positive thinking and thankfulness, you will position yourself for greater financial success.

As you adjust your mindset around money, you will not only enjoy financial freedom for yourself, but you will also be able to share that healthy, godly mindset with your children and others. One of the most powerful ways we can give back to others is to impart to them what we have learned. When our children and others know how to successfully earn an income and manage their money, they will be independent, free, thankful, and generous.

A healthy financial mindset is an incredible gift that will further God's kingdom and bless their lives. What a tremendous, blessed legacy to leave behind!

Always Keep Sight of Your Purpose

Finally, remember that the proper use of finances comes down to one word—purpose. Your God-given purpose should always guide you in the decisions you make about your work, income, savings, spending, and giving.

Consider Solomon as an example. The Bible tells us that he was vastly wealthy, yet he continued to prosper even more during his lifetime. God gave him the ability to grow and increase, so successfully that the Queen of Sheba was astounded at the richness of His kingdom. And God still considered him a godly man, as He was seeking the Lord.

Yet he lost his way and forgot about his purpose—which was to lead his nation in a godly way and lead others to the Lord. He focused instead on other, temporary things like women and gain, rather than on seeking the Lord. For many years, he lost his sense of fulfillment until he realized at the end of his life that God was the source of all his wealth, for the purpose of doing good.

We can learn from this example. As long as we diligently put the Lord first in our lives, He will lead us to make good decisions about every area—spiritual, emotional, relationships, physical health, career and ministry, and our finances. And as we follow His leading, we'll find ourselves achieving greater balance in our life and gaining more success in every area. Before we know it, we'll look back and see how we have been miraculously transformed by the godly changes we have made to our thinking and our actions.

And we'll be well on our way to walking out the great destiny He has for us. There is no greater blessing than that! May you rejoice in all He has done for you and is continuing to do for you—as you are continually transformed more and more into His image!

Day 1

Finances
Wealth Is of God

*"You shall remember the Lord your God,
for it is he who gives you power to get wealth, that he may confirm
his covenant that he swore to your fathers, as it is this day."*
—**Deuteronomy 8:18 (NKJV)**

God guided the Israelites and disciplined them for their good. He humbled them in the wilderness so that He might test the state of their heart and affections toward him. We are to be entirely dependent on God in all areas. God blesses our finances but expects us to realize where they came from and to use our financial means to glorify Him.

Gain Insight

Answer the questions, be honest with yourself and be transformed!

1. How has God blessed you financially in the past?

1. In what ways did you neglect to honor God with your wealth at that time?

2. In what ways will you honor and recognize God by giving your wealth now and in the future?

3. What are some of the ways you plan to learn more about managing your money?

4. Do others see God in you when they see your wealth? In what ways?

Pray

Thank You, Lord, that You have been faithful to me all my life. I am so grateful that You have given me the ability to make money. I realize, Lord, that everything comes from you. Show me, Lord, exactly how to manage my money so I will glorify You and bring others to You through the wealth You give to me. Help me to always give back to You everything and willingly surrender all for Your glory.

Day 2

Finances
Avoid Idolatry

*"Don't be obsessed with money but live content with what you have,
for you always have God's presence. For hasn't he promised you,
'I will never leave you, never! And I will not loosen my grip on your life!'"*
—**Hebrews 13:5 (TPT)**

Money is for our benefit, but we are never to place it before God! We must always love God more than money! As we do, we can expect to enjoy His presence with us and His overflowing blessings.

Gain Insight

Answer the questions, be honest with yourself and be transformed!

1. What are some of the ways you have chased after money more than God?

2. In what ways can you keep yourself free from the love of money?

3. Can you have nice things and still place God first? In what ways?

4. How can you think differently about money and make it obedient to you?

5. When others see you, will they see your love for God or your love for money? In what ways?

Pray

Lord, You are my first love! I thank You for everything that You have given to me! I know that all that I have comes from You. Help me to use all my material possessions for Your glory and to build up Your kingdom. Let thoughts of You be the first thing on my mind. I worship You, Lord, alone! Nothing shall come before You.

Day 3

Finances
Generosity

*"Give generously and generous gifts will be given back to you,
shaken down to make room for more. Abundant gifts will pour out upon you
with such an overflowing measure that it will run over the top!
The measurement of your generosity becomes the measurement of your return."*
— **Luke 6:38 (TPT)**

Our financial wellness includes both give and take, earning and paying out, saving and giving. And God's Word makes it clear that a generous heart not only blesses others, but also opens ways for provision and increase to come back to us.

Gain Insight

Answer the questions, be honest with yourself and be transformed!

1. How has God been generous with you?

2. What are some of the ways you have been generous with others?

3. In what ways would you like to be more generous?

4. In what ways will your generosity come back to you?

5. In what ways can you use wisdom in your generosity?

Pray

Lord, You have been so generous with me. I see You in everything that I have and all that I get to do. Give me a generous heart like Yours. Help me to see the needs of others and to meet those needs with wisdom. Thank You for all that You have given to me, Lord.

Day 4

Finances
Thoughts and Triggers

*"Don't be pulled in different directions or worried about a thing.
Be saturated in prayer throughout each day, offering your faith-filled requests
before God with overflowing gratitude. Tell him every detail of your life."*
—**Philippians 4:6 (TPT)**

Finding financial freedom and being transformed in this area of life will come as you gain greater awareness on how you think about money and wealth. Often, we learn what is untrue from our families, who may not have known what God says about finances and abundant provision. As you grow in the understanding of your own attitudes, you can begin to make the shifts necessary to free you up for greater financial growth.

Gain Insight

Answer the questions, be honest with yourself and be transformed!

1. What are some of the negative ways you have been programmed about money?

2. In what ways can you reprogram your mind with God's truth and peace?

3. What are some of the promises God gives to you about provision?

4. What are some of the words and phrases you will use to anchor yourself in Christ's provision?

5. In what ways can you keep your focus on God?

Pray

Lord, show me where I have thought negatively about money and have gained unhealthy patterns. Help me to stay focused on You and Your promises for my provision. Give me a heart of contentment and peace. Give me a mind that speaks to me with words that You would say—that I am blessed, content, successful and wealthy beyond measure. Thank You, Lord, for giving me great success.

Day 5

Finances
Honor God

"Glorify God with all your wealth, honoring him with your firstfruits, with every increase that comes to you. Then every dimension of your life will overflow with blessings from an uncontainable source of inner joy!"
—**Proverbs 3:9–10 (TPT)**

As we grow in our finances, we are to remember that God Himself is the Source of every good and perfect gift He has for us—including His provision. He has blessed us already in so many ways through Jesus Christ! When we give back to His kingdom through our giving and charitable efforts, we honor who He is and what He has done for us. It makes it possible for His kingdom to grow. And it will bless you too!

Gain Insight

Answer the questions, be honest with yourself and be transformed!

1. What are your beliefs about tithing to God? Have you practiced those beliefs?

   _____
   _____
   _____

2. What are some of the new ways you would like to think about tithing?

   _____
   _____
   _____

3. What will be your routine to budget and manage your money?

   _____
   _____

4. What are God's promises for honoring Him with the first tenth of your income?

5. What are some of the things you can do to trust God more for provision?

Pray

Lord, I seek to honor You with the first tenth of my income. Help me to set aside time to budget, to pray and to seek you for help in managing my money. Teach me Your ways and help me to be successful in all that I do. Help me to trust You more and to focus on Your promises for my provision.

Week Seven: Finances

Day 6

Finances
Legacy

"You shall love the Lord your God with all your heart and with all your soul and with all your might. And these words that I command you today shall be on your heart. You shall teach them diligently to your children, and shall talk of them when you sit in your house, and when you walk by the way, and when you lie down, and when you rise."
—Deuteronomy 6:5–7 (ESV)

When we are transformed in our finances, one of the most amazing blessings that comes about is the ability to leave an inheritance for our loved ones and to those in our community that God desires us to influence for good. Leaving a legacy behind is then a blessing we get the privilege of doing. How will you bless others with what you have gained and learned?

Gain Insight

Answer the questions, be honest with yourself and be transformed!

1. What are some of the ways you want to be remembered concerning your finances?

   _____
   _____
   _____

2. What are some of the lessons you will teach your children about money?

   _____
   _____
   _____

3. What are some of the things you can do to exemplify godly money management?

4. What are some of the godly thoughts you will impart to your children about money?

5. In what ways can you help your children to honor God with their wealth?

Pray

Thank You, Jesus, for helping me to break any generational curses pertaining to money. Help me to be a godly example to my children and future grandchildren and all those that I influence. Help me to think correctly about wealth and to pass on godly thoughts and ways to all who follow me. Thank You, Jesus, for allowing me to be a model of success for others to follow.

Day 7

Finances
Rest

*"You will sleep like a baby, safe and sound—
your rest will be sweet and secure."*
—**Proverbs 3:24 (TPT)**

Even in the area of finances, resting in the Lord is vital. After doing all we can do to care for our finances—including budgeting, learning about finances, saving, and more—we are to take a final step: We are to trust the Lord. As we put our faith in Him for our provision and seek Him to help meet our needs, the anxious cares we have will lessen, and we can find rest and peace as we walk out His will in the area of our finances.

Gain Insight

Answer the questions, be honest with yourself and be transformed!

1. In what ways does having peace about finances allow you to rest?

2. What can you do throughout your week to prepare to rest your mind about finances?

3. In what ways can you be thankful and receive more rest?

4. How does your generosity bring peace and rest to your mind?

5. In what ways does thinking victoriously allow you to have a restful mind?

Pray

Lord, help me to be aware of anything that gets in the way of my rest and sleep. Help me manage my finances in a way that is pleasing to You and furthers Your kingdom. Help me to trust You and to lean on You for my provision and peace. Give me deep sleep and plenty of rest for my days ahead.

Week Seven: Finances

Reflection for the Week on Finances

Answer the questions, be honest with yourself and be transformed!

1. Are you moving closer to your financial goals?

2. Is there anything getting in the way?

3. Do you need to set any new plans?

4. Have you found an accountability partner?

5. In what ways can you help someone in their financial life?

Write Your Inner Narration

Using what you have learned from this chapter, the scriptures you have memorized this week, and what you discovered while answering this week's questions, build on your original narration from weeks 1, 2, 3, 4, 5, and 6, and write an additional short godly narration using only positive words. If you find it helpful, review your answers to the daily questions from this week, take note of any positive words, and include them in your new godly narration for this week.

Example: I AM beautiful. I AM loved by God, just as I AM.
I AM forgiven. I AM pleasing to God. I AM strong. I AM courageous.

I AM filled with godly purpose. I AM equipped and able to achieve my godly goals.
I AM a son or a daughter of the King. I AM covered in His grace.
Nothing anyone says or does can harm me because I AM protected.

I AM healthy in my boundaries. I AM forgiving. I AM loved in my relationships.
I AM wise and gracious in my interactions with others in my life.

I AM emotionally well, I AM focused. I AM at peace and rested. I AM balanced.
I AM aware of what I feel and I AM led by God in how to respond to my emotions.

I AM strong in my body. I AM led by God in what to eat and drink for my health and well-being.
I make time for exercise and rest because I AM caring for my body, which is the temple of the Holy Spirit.

I AM passionate about fulfilling God's purpose in my career and/or ministry.
I AM filled with purpose and focus as I work and volunteer my time. I AM equipped to be successful in my job.

I AM a wise and godly steward of the finances God has given me.
I AM confident in His provision, as He is the Source of my blessings.
I AM trusting in Him because He meets all my needs according to His riches in glory by Christ Jesus… etc.

A Final Word

I am so thankful to my Lord, Jesus Christ, for transforming every area of my life and allowing me the opportunity to walk this journey of growth and godly change with you! God is so good! He is faithful! As you continue to become more like Him and see your own personal goals being accomplished, you'll be able to bless others through the blessings you have received. You'll be in a wonderful position to leave a meaningful and lasting legacy of the great victory found through trusting in Jesus Christ!

Your story will merge with the greatest story of all, which is the story of Jesus Christ and His great love and sacrifice for all! Your purpose and mission in life will be to help others come to know the great life found in Him.

If at any time you need an additional word of prayer, don't hesitate to reach out to our ministry team at info@YKIcoaching.com or LaVonne@LaVonneEarl.com. Each and every one of us, including myself, need others to care for us and to encourage us here on this earth. If you need someone to remind you of your worth and to help you with your narration of who you are in Christ, my team and I are here for you!

God has not asked you to take this journey of life alone. He has equipped you with His body, and we are here to serve you! God will give you the strength you need, and He will complete all He has in store for you, which is very, very good.

I love you, my fellow believer, and I am praying for you and your transformation in Christ! God bless you and keep you!

— La Vonne Earl

Appendix

Additional Tips on Self-Evaluation and Questions

The questions contained in this book are simply a starting point to help you guide yourself as you check in with the Lord and learn practical ways to search your heart, so that you can be transformed from Glory to Glory. Here, you will find some additional questions that may be beneficial to you. Feel free to use them as you see fit.

Keep in mind also that any of the questions contained in this book can be expanded on to help you grow. For example, if you find a question in the spirituality section and decide that it can apply also to another area of your life, such as finances, you have the freedom to do so.

Or you may find that as you begin to answer a question, a follow-up question comes to your mind. That is natural, because the Holy Spirit will bring things to your mind that will aid you in your self-discovery and transformation. As He brings additional questions and ideas to your attention, answer them as well. Allow Him to help you grow more and more every day!

Other questions are available in my book *A Coach for Christ*, which is a wonderful reference tool for all Christians. There are literally limitless questions that can help you grow, and I encourage you to consider purchasing a copy of *A Coach for Christ* so you can continue to coach yourself into greater and greater transformational growth in the Lord, as well as become equipped to help others grow in their relationship with the Lord.

In addition to asking great questions, it's valuable to find ways to keep track of your progress over time. There are many ways to do so—such as journaling, or even giving yourself a weekly check-in "rating" from 1 to 10 in each of the six areas of the Circle. There does not need to be any judgment attached to these numbers you are giving yourself. This is simply a handy way to recognize where you are at right now, and it gives you a way to look back and see how you were doing in that area a week, a month, even a year ago. Many people find this ability to track their progress greatly encouraging.

I personally rate myself deeply once a year to see how my life has changed. I like to keep my numbers high, around 8-9. And I know there is always room for improvement, so I never give myself a 10. It's a powerful way to see how far I have come and contemplate what I would like to accomplish next. And I encourage you to find a similar practice that does the same for you.

1. How would you describe your spirituality? (You may wish to assign yourself a number on a scale of 1 to 10, or you may write a short description of what your spiritual life is like at this particular moment in time.)

2. What are your spiritual beliefs, routines, and practices right now?

3. Is there anyone in your life who conflicts with your beliefs?

4. How do you feel about God? What kind of relationship do you have with Him? For example, is it easy or hard for you to talk with the Lord?

5. What are your spiritual plans and dreams?

6. Who are your closest relationships, and how would you describe them?

7. How much effort do you put into each of these relationships? In what ways would you like to improve these relationships?

8. Is there anyone causing you grief? Is there anyone you need to spend less time with? Is there anyone you need to forgive, including yourself?

9. Do you have friends outside of family? Do you wish to add more friends to your circle?

10. What are your relationship plans and dreams?

11. How would you describe your emotional life?

12. What do you currently do to take care of yourself emotionally? For example, do you get outside regularly? Do you eat a regular diet? How is your sleep?

13. What spiritual practices do you do for your emotional health? For example, do you practice meditation, prayer, visualization, etc.?

14. What are your plans and dreams for your emotional wellness?

15. How would you describe yourself in terms of your physical wellness right now?

16. Do you consider yourself healthy?

17. Do you consider yourself an attractive person?

18. Are you physically attracted to your spouse?

19. Do you judge people based on their physical appearance? How does that affect you?

20. Do you have any routines to keep your physical health in good shape?

21. Would you like to create an exercise plan?

22. What types of exercise you like the most?

23. What is your diet like?

24. Do you have clear goals in terms of what you eat?

25. Would you like to create a plan for better eating habits?

26. What plans and dreams do you have for your physical wellness?

27. How would you rate your finances? What makes you say that?

28. Do you currently work with someone to help you with financial planning? If not, would you like to create specific financial goals?

29. What do you feel the purpose of your finances are?

30. Do you feel financially free, or tied up by your finances?

31. If you had all the money in the world, what would you do?

32. What plans and dreams do you have for your finances overall?

33. What plans and dreams do you have for your retirement?

34. Do you have a tithing or charity account?

35. What type of work, ministry and/or volunteering do you do? Do you see it as work you are doing for the Lord?

36. If you could do anything, what would you do? What do you feel your strengths and talents are? What are you passionate about?

37. Would you hire yourself? How would you like your work associates to remember you?

38. Do you enjoy the work and/or ministry you do? Are there things you might like to change?

39. Would you consider moving for a new job? Or perhaps taking courses?

40. What plans and dreams do you have for your career, volunteerism, and/or ministry?

Who I Am in Christ Scriptures

Adored	1 John 3:1	Helpful	Ephesians 4:32
Authentic	John 8:32	Holy	John 17:17
Beautiful	Ecclesiastes 3:11	Honorable	Romans 12:17
Brave	Philippians 4:13	Hopeful	2 Corinthians 5:6
Calm	Isaiah 43:2	Hospitable	1 Timothy 5:10
Capable	James 1:5	Humble	James 4:10
Caring	Galatians 6:10	Intelligent	James 3:13
Cheerful	1 Thessalonians 5:16–18	Inspired	1 Thessalonians 1:6
Comforting	2 Corinthians 1:3–4	Joyful	Psalm 5:11
Committed	Ruth 1:16–18	Kind	3 John 1:5
Compassionate	James 1:27	Leader	Psalm 18:43
Confident	Hebrews 4:16	Loved	John 13:34
Content	Hebrews 13:5	Loyal	2 Kings 18:6
Daughter	Galatians 3:26	Merciful	Psalm 30:4
Dedicated	Revelation 14:12	Modest	1 Timothy 5:2
Dependable	1 John 2:5–6	Motherly	John 15:12–13
Determined	2 Timothy 4:7	Non-Judgmental	Matthew 7:1
Disciple	Isaiah 50:4	Nurturing	1 Peter 5:2
Disciplined	1 Peter 1:13	Obedient	Isaiah 1:19
Discreet	Proverbs 8:12	Passionate	1 Peter 3:13
Edifying	Romans 15:2	Patient	Proverbs 14:29
Energetic	Romans 12:8	Peaceful	Proverbs 3:17
Faithful	Psalm 23:6	Persevering	Psalm 51:10
Flexible	2 Timothy 2:15	Persuasive	1 Corinthians 9:20
Focused	Psalm 91:14	Positive	Proverbs 18:20
Free	2 Corinthians 3:17	Powerful	2 Timothy 1:7
Friend	Proverbs 17:17	Prayerful	1 Thessalonians 5:17
Full of Light	Matthew 6:22	Prepared	Philippians 1:10
Full of Love	Philippians 1:9	Productive	Proverbs 21:5
Fun	Ecclesiastes 5:18–20	Protective	John 15:13
Generous	Psalm 37:21	Proud	1 Corinthians 1:31
Good	1 Timothy 4:4	Pure	Philippians 4:8
Grace-Filled	2 Thessalonians 3:18	Quiet	Exodus 14:14
Grateful	Psalm 66:8	Relatable	1 Corinthians 9:20
Great Listener	Exodus 19:5	Reliable	Proverbs 12:5
Grounded	Ephesians 3:17	Resourceful	Isaiah 41:10
Happy	Psalm 9:2	Responsible	1 Timothy 5:8
Hard-Working	Proverbs 10:4	Reverent	Titus 2:3

Romantic . . . . Genesis 2:18
Royal . . . . James 2:8
Self-Controlled . . . . . . 2 Peter 1:6
Selfless . . . . Mark 12:33
Sense of Humor . . . . . Proverbs 31:25–26
Servant . . . . 2 Timothy 1:3
Simple . . . . James 5:12
Skilled . . . . Proverbs 16:16
Soft . . . . Proverbs 25:15
Son . . . . Romans 8:14
Strong . . . . Philippians 4:13
Successful . . . . Romans 8:28
Supportive . . . . Hebrews 10:24–25
Sweet . . . . Psalm 133:1

Tender . . . . 1 Peter 3:8
Thankful . . . . Psalm 100:4
Thoughtful . . . . Philippians 4:10
Tolerant . . . . Colossians 3:13
Transparent . . . . Philippians 1:10
True . . . . 3 John 1:3
Trusting . . . . Proverbs 30:5
Understanding . . . . . 1 Kings 2:3
Victorious . . . . Romans 8:37
Virtuous . . . . Proverbs 31:10
Warrior . . . . 1 John 5:4
Wholesome . . . . Ephesians 4:29
Wise . . . . Ecclesiastes 7:12

A Salvation Prayer

Dear Lord Jesus, I come to You humbly and confess that I am a sinner. I believe You died for my sins and rose from the dead, so that I could be set free from my sins. Please forgive me. I turn from my sins right now. I believe that You are Lord and Savior, and I am asking you to be mine. Come into my heart and life right now. I want to trust and follow You. Thank You for forgiving me and giving me a new life, in You. Amen.

Example Narration for Godly Anchoring

Through godly anchoring, we are seeking to align our character with who Jesus Christ is and who He says we are. I am only these things because Jesus Christ, my Lord and savior, is the great I AM. He goes before me. He perfects me. It is because of Him that I have peace and complete wholeness. Remember that pride goes before a fall (Proverbs 16:18). We must be careful when we anchor ourselves to do so in Christ and to give all honor, praise, and glory to Him. This is why I capitalize I AM—it is recognizing who is causing me to become these things, Jesus Christ, the Great I AM.

The list of scriptures and positive words you can use to create your anchoring narration is endless, as God has so many good things to bless you with! Continue to add to your narration as God gives you His words.

There may be times where you do not say the entire list over yourself in your prayer time, and that is okay. But consistency is key. Bless yourself in the Lord at least in the morning and at night before bed. Just a few words are all that are needed. Read through your entire list at least once a week and watch how it grows! God says that He who is faithful with little will be faithful with much! (Luke 16:10) Be faithful with the little words He starts you with, and He will continue to give you more!

Add to your list characteristics you would like to possess and proclaim them over yourself with confidence! Remember, God called Gideon a "Mighty Warrior" when he was hiding in the wheat threshing floorm (Judges 6:12). This is how God blesses us into who we are to become! You will get used to this new way of speaking about yourself, and begin to bless not only yourself into your true identity and character, but you also will bless others around you into their true identity.

I like to place my essential oil on my bathroom sink along with my Godly Narration list. This way, I see it when I brush my teeth twice a day and can easily start reading the list as part of my habitual spiritual practice. When I was first learning this method of blessing myself through Christ into my healing and wholeness, I kept this list with me throughout the day. I added it to my phone and looked at it all day until I was well enough to just keep the habit of twice a day.

Appendix

Here's an example of what my own narration looks like:

*I AM a daughter of the King. I AM beautiful and loved.
I AM a woman of strength and mighty valor, full of wealth and wisdom.
I AM courageous. I AM completely healed and victorious because Jesus has redeemed me and my life.*

*I AM pure. I AM confident. I AM blessed beyond measure. I AM forgiven, and therefore I forgive others.
I AM filled with God's love, which I freely give.*

*I AM wise and discerning. I have healthy boundaries that protect me and my family.
I AM dedicated and loyal, flexible, and moved by the Holy Spirit. I trust and know that God
has great plans for me. I read and obey His Word, the Bible. I know my Heavenly Father has
many things He wants to say to me and teach me. I AM a good listener, and I love to learn.*

*I AM hard-working, and I AM also able to rest. I AM balanced.
I AM able to do all things through Christ who gives me strength. I AM creative and resourceful.*

*I AM kind and gentle with others, full of God's grace. I AM a shining light to all around me.
I AM generous to the poor and seek ways continually to bless others. I AM able to bless and pray for my enemies.*

I handle my trials with grace, as I know God works everything out for my good. I AM filled with joy!

*I AM very passionate about life, and the Good News of the Gospel! I seek to share it with
others. I teach with wisdom and kindness as loving instruction pours from my lips.*

*I watch over and protect my household. Love permeates my home. My children love the Lord,
and they will forever stay close to Him and teach their children and grandchildren to love God.*

*I AM successful in all that I do. I AM relatable to others. I AM fun to be around.
I laugh easily and bring out the good in others. I AM a great mom, and my children love me.*

*I AM centered on Christ. I AM focused. I AM easy-going. I AM physically healthy and enjoy
taking care of myself. I AM happy and at peace. I AM stable, and I have a sound mind.*

*I AM content in all circumstances. I AM grateful for all my blessings.
I AM deeply loved by God, and I AM never alone.*

Thank You, Jesus, for being with me every moment of the day! I love You, Lord.

God Sees You as Beautiful and Loved!

My friend, this powerful, positive, life-giving narration isn't just for me. It is true for you as well. As a son or daughter of the King, you are greatly loved, and so much more!

I am so thankful to have had the opportunity to be your coach for these seven weeks as you have become more transformed into the image of Christ. Really, we could say you have become unveiled, revealing who you have been all along!

God bless you, my friend! Please keep in touch!

La Vonne

Resources and References

A Coach for Christ
by La Vonne Earl

Born to Bloom:
Complete Healing from Any Form of Sexual Abuse
by La Vonne Earl

The Daniel Plan:
40 Days to a Healthier Life
by Daniel Amen, Mark Hyman, and Rick Warren

Who I Am in Christ
by Neil T. Anderson

Feelings Buried Never Die
by Karol K. Truman

Saying What's Real:
7 Keys to Authentic Communication and Relationship Success
by Susan Campbell

The Total Money Makeover
by Dave Ramsey

The Passion Translation New Testament
with Psalms, Proverbs, and Song of Songs
by Brian Simmons

Prayers from the Throne Room:
365 Daily Meditations and Declarations
by Brian Simmons

Made in the USA
Las Vegas, NV
30 July 2025

25587032R00129